Life After Dentistry

Retirement Lifestyle Readiness

ALAN ROADBURG, Ph.D.

SecondCareer
RETIREMENT PROGRAM

About the Author

Dr. Alan Roadburg is the founder and President of the Second Career Program. He has a unique blend of academic and practical experience and has literally written the book on retirement lifestyle education. He earned a Ph.D. (Sociology) from the University of Edinburgh and was a tenured Professor at Dalhousie University (1978 - 1985), and an Adjunct Professor at Simon Fraser University. His academic experience includes teaching courses in Social Gerontology (the study of aging), The Sociology of Retirement, Social Psychology, Sociology of Work, and Leisure Studies. Dr. Roadburg conducted several major research projects on retirees, and has written extensively on the retirement experience.

Alan changed careers in 1986 and developed the Second Career Program. Specializing in lifestyle retirement planning, he has conducted hundreds of retirement workshops with literally thousands of pre and post retirees and has developed a strong understanding of the unique needs of today's retirees. In short, he has been able to integrate his extensive research experience on retirees, with many years of hands-on workshop experience. His unique approach views retirement as a second career, resulting in an entirely different way of planning for retirement. *Life After Dentistry* is the self-help version of Dr. Roadburg's workshop along with the results of research among 312 retired dentists.

Roadburg, Alan

Life After Dentistry

ISBN 978-0-9811740-5-1

1. Retirement - Lifestyle, non-financial. 2. Dentistry. 3. Self-help
I. Title

Second Career Retirement Program

Books in this series may be customized and purchased in quantities. For details contact the Sales Department at admin@lifegoal.net, or call 905-764-9494

Contents

Part 3 / LIFE GOAL PLANNING WORKSHOP....177

Acknowledgements

I want to express my gratitude to the many people who directly and indirectly helped make this book a reality. My appreciation extends back to the thousands of people who attended my retirement planning workshops over the years. Their participation and feedback enabled me to develop, test and improve a Life Goal Planning approach to retirement planning.

A special thank you is extended to the retired and semi-retired dentists who took part in the research that is incorporated throughout this book. They are the true experts on 'life after dentistry' and their advice and experiences are a welcome addition.

Finally, I want to thank the Association of Retiring Dentists and Dr. Neil Hitunen who became a major part of this project right from the very beginning. His input during the design and implementation of the questionnaire, as well as the final edit of this book, were invaluable.

If situations are defined as real,
they are real in their consequences.
(W.I. Thomas, 1923)

INTRODUCTION

There are two forms of spending in retirement - time and money, and there are two forms of planning for retirement - lifestyle and financial planning. These distinct planning procedures complement and enhance each other, but at the same time, they are worlds apart. One major difference is financial planning is based on an established body of knowledge and most financial advisors are highly trained accredited professionals. However things are different on the non-financial or lifestyle planning side. Lifestyle planning involves identifying how you want to spend the rest of your life after you retire and anyone can claim to be an expert in this area. There are no formal training requirements or accreditation standards, and it is common to see books and web sites in this area written by people with a vast array of backgrounds and experience including financial planners, career planners, social workers, medical professionals, and retirees, who suddenly become experts in retirement lifestyle planning.

The Traditional Approach

The history of retirement lifestyle planning reveals why these problems occur. Being a relatively new field that started to emerge in the 1950's, and motivated by a concern for employee welfare following retirement, a handful of major corporations called on health care professionals to develop programs to help employees through the transition at the end of their careers. Retirement was viewed simply as giving up work and the solutions related more to the symptoms rather than the cause of any problems. Because health professionals created the early programs, the traditional approach tended to address issues that related to aging rather than to retirement. So issues such as health and safety, nutrition, recreation, stress management, hobbies, travel, sex and aging, prepaid funerals, and so on, formed the basis of the traditional approach to retirement lifestyle planning.

As a body of knowledge, retirement lifestyle planning is not grounded in solid research or theory, it is full of generalizations and value judgments, and it usually proposes a one-size-fits all or 'cookie-cutter' solution. Most retirement lifestyle planning authors today add their own spin and recycle the original outdated approach because it has always been done that way. So why re-invent the wheel? The answer is simple. The wheel is broken. The Boomers are retiring, they are the architects of a new retirement as they re-create retirement in their own image, and their main concerns are not adequately addressed by the traditional approach.

A New Approach

I am not a financial planner and my interest in retirement planning evolved from an earlier interest in the Sociology of Occupations and Professions. During my Ph.D. graduate work in Scotland at the University of Edinburgh, I was interested in the Sociology of Work and Leisure and carried out research on this topic by focusing on a single activity that some people pursued as work and that others pursued as leisure. My fieldwork involved participant observation research among professional and amateur soccer players to discern differences in the work and leisure experience surrounding the same activity. I spent four months participating in the day-to-day training and social activities of a professional soccer club (based in Edinburgh) as well as two amateur teams. I supplemented this with in-depth personal interviews among professional and amateur gardeners.

When I obtained a university teaching position, I wanted to extend my interest in meanings of work and leisure to focus on people who were not working. I chose retirees. This research involved in-depth interviews with 352 retirees looking at work, leisure, friendships, and life satisfaction, and published the results in my book entitled Aging: Retirement, Leisure, and Work. [(1)]

Several main findings emerged from my early research experiences. First, regarding perceptions of work and leisure, when people are working they tend to view leisure as time off work or free time. However, when they retire, because most of their time is free time, they tend to view leisure as pleasurable or enjoyable activities. Therefore, retirement is not leisure. Second, when asked what they missed from work, the three most frequently mentioned items were social contact, having something to do, and daily routine. Interestingly, only 9% of the males and 2% of the females mentioned money as something they missed from work. This is not to suggest that money isn't important - far from it. This does however suggest that when people retire, they adapt to their financial situation and if they identify areas to improve, they focus on the non-financial domain. Finally, the finding that had the greatest influence on the direction of my work in this areas was, if people have problems in retirement they most likely stem from boredom.

After six years of university teaching and research, I changed careers to concentrate full time on conducting retirement lifestyle planning workshops. Following my research experiences, my initial challenge was to develop a program to help people replace satisfactions like social contact, having something to do, and a daily routine no longer provided by work. Having rejected the traditional model as not effective in this regard and working with insights from the career change literature, I created a new approach called ***Life Goal Planning.*** My career change from the university to conducting retirement lifestyle workshops took place over 20 years ago and ***Life Goal Planning*** has been repeatedly tested, refined, and improved through the years.

In this sense, this book bridges the gap between theory and practice. It originated in academic research and theory (my own and others), and developed and was perfected through hands-on and practical experience with thousands of pre- and post-retirees who attended and provided feedback on my workshops over the years. The result is not another spin on the traditional approach, but a new paradigm or frame of reference in retirement lifestyle preparation.

Clearly, retirement today is not what it used to be. It is changing to reflect the emergence of a new breed of retirees, the baby boomers. The boomers will live longer, retire richer, are more highly educated, and will expect more from life in retirement compared to any previous group of retirees. The main purpose of this book is to provide you with the tools and insights to ensure your retirement will be worthwhile and enjoyable. I must warn you at the outset, these tools do not focus on the financial domain, and they will not help you increase your nest egg or reduce taxes. Most people equate retirement planning with financial planning but as this book will make clear, financial planning is a necessary but not sufficient condition for retirement happiness. In fact, I would argue that financial planning is not retirement planning, it is money management. Moreover, because you will be spending both time and money in retirement, you will have to manage and integrate both elements. If it is not already obvious, the secret to retirement happiness lies beyond the financial realm.

Of course, money is important but during my work with retirees I have met many people who are well off financially, but who do not enjoy retirement, and I have met people who are just getting by financially but consider retirement as the best years of their lives. This fact points to one undeniable conclusion - money alone will not guarantee retirement happiness. It is unfortunate that most people do not think about planning for the non-financial side of retirement because they think things will look after themselves. On the other hand, if they look for help, the standard or traditional approach to retirement lifestyle planning does not adequately prepare people to answer the most important question of all; how do you plan to spend your time for the rest of your life?

Another important element that distinguishes this book is I strive to avoid value judgments and generalizations. My goal is not to suggest or tell you what to do, but simply to provide you with the tools to identify and create your own retirement that you will consider enjoyable, worthwhile, and purposeful. Creating a retirement that will be worthwhile and enjoyable is probably not going to appear magically. However, if you are prepared to expand your horizons and use your imagination, think creatively, and do a little work, you will reach this goal.

Your Retirement Mentors

Retirement is a unique experience and it means different things to different people. The problem is, most retirement lifestyle authors tend to ignore this fact by presenting what they feel are the necessary ingredients for retirement happiness, based on the author's own experience in retirement, or on a few case studies. Underlying this somewhat narrow perspective, is an outdated notion of retirement based mainly on earlier work in this field by health professionals where the emphasis was on what I call the "what to look out for" approach.

In addition, the type of profession or occupation you retire from, can influence the way you approach and experience retirement. Clearly retiring from dentistry can involve different considerations compared to retiring from other lines of work. To overcome these biases, I went to the experts. After all, who would know better about retiring from dentistry than dentists who are retired? I created the ***Life After Dentistry*** online survey and received 312 replies from retired physicians. The subjects were located through the ADA and The Association of Retiring Dentists (www.retiringdentists.com). I refer to the research subjects as 'retirement mentors'. A mentor is a trusted counselor or teacher, and your retirement mentors include dentists with retirement experience.

You will notice that only 34% of the respondents classified themselves as fully retired. This is a a result of two possible factors. First, many of the respondents were located through the Association of Retiring Dentists, and these individuals were for the most part not totally retired. Another important consideration is that it is relatively easy for dentists to in a sense ease into retirement by working progressively a few days a week, either continuing with their current practice, teaching, or other dental related activities.

Your Retirement Mentors
Sample Size 312

Gender
Male..........90%
Female......10%

Current Age
<58...............5%
58-64..........29%
65-71..........49%
>72 +.........17%

Marital Status
Married....................................87%
Widowed....................................3%
Never Married.............................3%
Separated/Divorced....................5%
Common Law/Partnership......2%

Health Status
Excellent................45%
Very Good.............39%
Good......................15%
Poor..........................1%

Type of Practice[1]
General...................86%
Specialty.................12%
Solo........................18%
Group.....................16%

Current Participation in Dentistry[2]
Totally retired.......34%
Semi-retired...........66%

Length of time Retired/Semi-Retired
0-5 years.................73%
6-10 years...............14%
11+ years................13%

1. Exceeds 100% as some indicated multiple choices.
2. Semi-Retired involves working in dentistry an average of 3 days a week. For example,

> *I work as a dentist 2 to 3 days per week. However I take a week off for travel almost every 6 to 8 weeks.*
>
> *About two hours every two weeks every 2 to 3 weeks on friends who request to be seen as new patients.*

Work as a consultant with an insurance company.

License is still active, I do humanitarian missions once a year.

You will also notice that only 10% of our respondents were women. This reflects the fact that traditionally dentistry has been a male dominated profession. For example, according to the ADA Health Policy Institute, in 1978, only 15.9 percent of first-year dental students were women. In 2014, it was 47.7 percent. (ADA News, *Women in dentistry see progress, continued challenges*, January 18, 2016). Presumably if we were to conduct this research in the future we would have a far greater percentage of retired women dentists respond to the survey.

Life After Dentistry Questionnaire

The questionnaire (reproduced at the end of the book) included both closed and open-ended questions and covered the main issues that can affect retirement happiness. These included the decision to retire, type and degree of retirement planning, working in retirement, volunteer activities, moving after retirement, friendships, spousal relations, and overall satisfaction in retirement. The respondents were also given the opportunity to express their opinions freely on the main attractions and drawbacks of retirement, and they were asked what advice they would give to other dentists contemplating retirement.

Closed-ended questions provide possible answers and in some cases, they can only choose one, for example gender, or age at retirement. In other cases, they can choose as many as they like, such as reasons for retiring. In this case, the totals will often be greater than 100% as most chose multiple replies. Open ended questions, such as advantages, drawbacks, and advice on retirement, resulted in qualitative responses where the subjects were free to express their feeling through written responses. To give structure or order to the open-ended responses, each response was evaluated and in the process, we identified general categories based on the type of response. This process enabled us to determine percentages of respondents in each category, and due to the opportunity for multiple responses, totals exceed 100%.

This type of research can have its limitations. It is possible that those people who felt strongly for or against retirement will be more likely to take the time to respond, or respond in a particular manner. In addition, because the research took place online, this could have excluded some people. Nevertheless, we were pleased with the response rate and the range of responses and I believe our sample accurately reflects the experiences and opinions of most retired dentists. The research results are woven into the information that follows, and to my knowledge Life After Dentistry is the only lifestyle planning program that includes input from such a large group of retied dentists.

Most of the issues included are relevant regardless of economic conditions. Because the respondents shared their experiences and advice for your benefit, this unique resource can be extremely valuable for your future retirement and you would be wise to learn from their experiences. My advice is that you view their experiences and comments with an open mind and consider them based on your situation and needs.

To Postpone or Rescue Your Retirement

Economic uncertainty can create a new set of retirement concerns. In a survey by AARP, a senior's advocacy group, 65% of workers over age 45 planned to delay retirement.(2) In a Canadian survey, 42% of respondents over 40 said they would postpone their retirement by an average of 5.9 years.(3) There is an old saying, 'you can't control the winds, but you can adjust your sails'. If you are considering postponing your retirement, you can take control and do something about your situation rather than just wait and hope for things to get better. ***Life Goal Planning*** will help you identify areas you can control or adjust in the non-financial domain, and will introduce you to various strategies for rescuing your retirement. It will give you an overall objective view of your future retirement plans or options in the context of your financial situation, to enable you to make a rational decision about your best plan of action. Of course, money is important, but there are things you can do and possible solutions found, by looking beyond the financial realm.

This book is not about how to save money during a financial crisis, or how to position your portfolio for a rebound. Nevertheless, if you are looking for a process that can point you in the right direction, and get you started on the right road, ***Life Goal Planning***, tested by thousands of pre and post retirees over the past 20+ years, can be your solution. Even if you decide to postpone your retirement, ***Life Goal Planning*** can offer some unexpected benefits. If you find yourself out of work and on the brink of retiring, if you don't have any options, it can provide some hope, guidance, and inspiration.

Link with Financial Planning

Early in my career, I realized that ***Life Goal Planning*** has an additional and very important benefit for retirement in that it can provide an integral element that is often missing from a financial plan. Typically, when I present my workshop I do so with a financial planner and in most, if not all cases, the planner stresses the importance of establishing a financial goal. In fact, according to the Financial Planning Association, "The financial planning profession exists to help people reach their financial goals and dreams."(4) The problem is, establishing a financial goal or dream is based on knowing how you want to spend your time in retirement and based on my 20 plus years of workshop experience, I would estimate that only about one-third of pre-retirees have a solid plan for retirement. Because ***Life Goal Planning*** can help you create worthwhile and enjoyable retirement plans, it can provide the missing element in personalizing your financial plan. The connection between Life Goal and Financial Planning is explained in more detail in Chapter 5.

Plan of the Book

In the first part of the book, you will find various concepts and issues presented through a collage of conversations. The purpose is to bring your image of retirement in line with reality and to make you aware of and provide insights into the key issues that can affect retirement happiness. Although the characters that you will meet are fictional, don't let the simple conversational style fool you. The issues, theories, ideas, concepts, and examples that we discuss are based on the real life experiences of various participants in my retirement workshops. We begin with an overview of several important concepts used throughout the book. I argue that the standard view of retirement is out of date, negative, and could actually be a counterproductive self-fulfilling prophecy. I present a new paradigm or frame of reference for retirement that is more compatible with the new breed of retirees. You will also learn the secret to retirement happiness.

Chapter 1 (Handyman) introduces a new way to look at retirement - including a full explanation of 'retire with a dash'. I use this opportunity to 'fix' or 'repair' the sometimes unknown, false image that surrounds retirement. This chapter outlines what retirement is or can be today, rather than what it was in the past. The Baby Boomers are facing a new retirement that requires a new perspective and guidelines.

Chapter 2 (Do You Want to Know a Secret?) reveals the secret to retirement happiness based on how you will be spending your time in retirement. It also includes a process to incorporate lifestyle and financial planning.

Chapter 3 (Ticket to Ride) is an overview of a unique process to guide your retirement career so it will be worthwhile and enjoyable. The outline of this process is in detail in Part 3, through a series of do-it-yourself exercises. You will learn how to evaluate your retirement plans, and maybe make them better, and how to come up with new ideas, should you need them. We also address the issue of what happens if you know what you want to do in retirement, but for some reason you can't do it. You will learn that you have an 'ace up your sleeve'.

Chapter Four (A Hard Day's Night) looks at working after retirement. I present several issues to think about including the question, "Are you taking the easy way out?"

Chapter 5 (Money Can't Buy Me Love) outlines the relationship between Life Goal and Financial Planning. Both planning methods complement and work in parallel with changes in one influencing changes in the other.

Chapter 6 (Did You Ever Have to Make Up Your Mind?) provides help with the decision to retire. Money is not the only consideration, and you will learn a few techniques to turn an otherwise subjective decision into an objective one.

Chapter 7 (When I'm Sixty-Four) is in response to a question raised by The Beatles over 40 years ago. I present an entirely different way of looking at aging and argue that it has absolutely nothing to do with retirement.

Chapter 8 (With a Little Help from My Friends) focuses on how retirement can affect a marriage relationship and friendships. It includes some real life examples of how problems can emerge, and how to deal with them. Of course, not everyone is married at retirement, so retaining and perhaps building new friendships can become even more important.

Chapter 9 (Our House) focuses on moving after you retire. We look at some potential problems and overcoming them. What happens if one person wants to move but the spouse doesn't? On the other hand, what happens if you move and later realize you made a mistake?

Part 3, includes the ***Life Goal Planning Workshop***, the defining element of this book, designed to help you find a life after work that will be worthwhile and enjoyable. This is a self-help version of the workshop that I have been delivering to clients for more than 20 years. It is not a magic one size fits all solution, because each person's solution to finding a worthwhile and enjoyable future lifestyle will be different. You will learn how to identify your life goal, how to evaluate your retirement plans, ways to improve them, and how to develop new activities and interests should you need them. You will also learn how to integrate your Life Goal with your financial plan, and ultimately how to guide your retirement career.

The ***Life Goal Planning Workshop*** is not designed as armchair or bedtime reading. You can complete the hands-on workshop on your own or with a small group. To understand and appreciate the value of ***Life Goal Planning***, you have to learn the process by completing the exercises. The process is presented in a generic mode and it is up to you to develop and put your plan into action. You will probably have to make a few adjustments across several retirement variables and, to see some results you are going to have to put in effort, keep your mind open to new insights and ideas, think, brainstorm, and experiment. You have to look for input from your friends, family, and perhaps a financial advisor, and it may take time.

I have purposefully excluded some topics that often appear in other retirement planning books, such as health tips, end of life resources, social services, retirement communities, or love and sex (sorry), from this book. Granted, these can be important, but they have nothing to do with the transition from work to retirement. In addition, I have dealt with some topics that are included from a slightly different perspective compared to what you may be expecting. For instance, we look at working in retirement and ask you the question: Are you taking the easy way out? As another example, I argue that aging has absolutely nothing to do with retirement. Although you will find this subject in most other books on retirement lifestyle planning, my approach and the way I develop it, is quite different. Realizing that friendship is a very important element, your retirement mentors have a lot to say on this matter. They also have some very good suggestions if you are considering moving after you retire. The issues, theories, ideas, concepts, and examples presented in the following pages are grounded in the real life experiences of various participants from my retirement workshops, and the results of the ***Life After Dentistry*** Survey.

For an idea of what lies ahead, several people who have attended my workshops have suggested I turn it into a board game. Although this idea is intriguing and it underscores how much they enjoyed the workshop, there are two problems with this suggestion. First, a board game is generally thought of as a frivolous diversion. ***Life Goal Dentistry*** is neither frivolous nor a diversion. Second, in a board game one person emerges as a winner and by default, the other players are losers. Because everyone who completes the ***Life Goal Planning*** exercises are winners, it does not lend itself to a board game. So rather than a board game, ***Life Goal Planning*** is presented in an easy to read workbook with self-help exercises to ensure that your retirement will be worthwhile and enjoyable.

Measure Your Retirement Lifestyle Readiness

Before you begin, I encourage you to complete the Retirement Lifestyle Readiness Quiz starting on page W-2 in your worksheets at the back of the book. After you complete the program, you can re-evaluate your lifestyle readiness to see how it has improved.

PART 1

The Key to Retirement Happiness

1

HANDYMAN

(James Taylor, 1977)

A New Frame of Reference

I am a bit of a handyman. I have not received training in this area, and I don't have elaborate or expensive tools. However, I enjoy doing odd jobs around the house. When a section of my fence blew down during the winter, I fixed it temporarily. It needed a more permanent repair as well as a fresh coat of paint. I picked up the necessary supplies to complete the job. The weather was no longer an excuse, it was sunny and hot, and I was outside fixing the fence when my neighbor Dave poked his head over the fence.

"Hi neighbor," he said. "What's up? Do you need any help?"

"No thanks," I replied. "I can finish this on my own. It's not a big job. After I fix this post I'm going to paint the fence."

"Well, then I'll help you paint," he said with a smile.

I could tell that Dave had something on his mind. His offer to help me paint my side of the fence confirmed that things were a little bit out of the ordinary. Dave and his wife Diane had been good neighbors over the years. We didn't see each other socially, but Dave and I often chatted as we worked in our yards and we had a good arrangement of lending each other tools. It was not usual for Dave to make such a generous offer, but I accepted his offer and told him that I would be ready to paint in about an hour.

"OK," he said. "I'll just go in to change and join you later." He headed for his house.

True to his word, Dave appeared with a paintbrush in hand, a stool to sit on, and dressed in his working clothes. He was serious about helping me with the fence. I couldn't help thinking about how Tom Sawyer had convinced his friend to paint Aunt Polly's fence.

We worked away quietly for a few minutes and then he said, "I have been wondering. I know you work with retirees and we have a bit of a problem. Diane suggested I talk to you. She said maybe you could help."

I had a good idea of what was on his mind. He was a dentist and Diane was a teacher. A while ago, he mentioned that he was starting to think about retiring and ever since, he kept making little remarks such as "Pretty soon I will be free as a bird." I had the feeling, however, that he was hiding his true concerns about retirement.

"What's the problem?" I asked.

"We talked about this before," he said, "but lately I have been thinking about retiring and last week Diane and I went to a retirement seminar put on by her school. It was quite, how should I put this, *an eye-opener.*"

"In what way?" I replied.

"Well mostly it was good, but I can't help feeling sort of scared. I have been practicing dentistry for more than thirty years and I like my work. I don't know if scared is the right word, but I am feeling uncertain about the future. I don't have to retire now. The problem is, I really don't know what to do."

"Do you remember my friend Les?" he asked.

"Not exactly," I replied.

"He retired about a year ago, and I think he is having real problems. Not money problems, he seems to be OK in that department. When he first retired, he kept telling me how busy he was. However, after a while it seems he ran out of things to do. In fact, he got quite depressed. I haven't seen him for a while and the last thing I want is to be like him with everyone feeling sorry for me."

To shift Dave's focus away from thinking about one bad example and to start thinking about retirement in general, I said, "I can understand your concern, Dave. After all, retiring can involve major changes in your life. The problem is we are trained and educated for most things in life, except retirement."

"That is so true," he replied. "I was hoping that the seminar would help, but it didn't. I'm still confused."

"Why don't you tell me about the seminar you and Diane attended," I suggested.

As Dave dipped his brush into the paint bucket he said, "Well, parts of it were pretty good. They talked about a lot of things, but all in all, at least for me, it was a bit of a downer."

I felt myself cringe because in all likelihood, the course he attended followed a traditional approach to retirement education that was common today and that I think is out of date.

What I call the traditional approach tends to present a false image of retirement based on a somewhat haphazard tradition. To be more specific, retirement lifestyle or non-financial planning is relatively new. It evolved from trial and error rather than basic, high-quality research. Motivated by a vague moral concern for employee welfare following retirement, a handful of major corporations began to develop programs in the 1950's to help employees through the transition awaiting them at the end of their working careers. People in the health professions developed the original approach to retirement education and the subjects covered reflected this orientation. The problems are, this model or approach is not based on properly formulated research. Some of the issues confuse retirement with aging. Many do not apply to everyone. They often include generalizations and subtle moral judgments about what you should or should not do in retirement.

I have seen statements such as; "You should always wait at least a year following retirement before making any changes in where to live," or, "For a happy and healthy retirement you should become involved in something completely different at least once a year", or "Do nothing for at least a year following retirement." Notwithstanding that, these generalizations contradict each other, whenever I come across personal opinions and judgments about what people should or should not do in retirement, I react negatively, and most important of all, they can't help Dave with his dilemma. That's why I cringed when Dave said the course he attended was a downer.

I asked him what the course covered and he replied, "Mostly they talked about financial matters. As I said, it was good. They had a few speakers and some of them, especially the financial guy, really knew his stuff. Diane and I have a financial planner who has been advising us for a long time so most of what he talked about we already knew."

"Did they go through other issues besides money?" I asked.

"That was part of the problem," he replied. "They talked about retirement being the best time of your life. They referred to it as the golden years. They don't look too golden to me. Anyway, the guy said that we would have an extra gazillion hours to fill in retirement and he gave a few examples of people who retired and what they were doing. One speaker talked about an organization for seniors, I don't remember what it was called, where they travel and study."

"Do you mean Elderhostel?" I asked.

"Yes, that's it. But to tell you the truth, I'm not interested in that."

Dave put down his brush and said, "Actually, I have the course description in the house. I can't remember all the details. Should I get it?"

"Sure," I replied. "I'm curious to see what they covered."

He returned with the course description and I could see by the topics included that it followed the traditional approach I referred to above.

"Do you want my opinion of the course?" I asked.

"Why not," he said. "You're the expert."

I suppressed my true feelings about the traditional model and said, "Looking only at the non-financial side, I have a problem with some of the contents."

"A problem?" he replied with a puzzled look on his face.

"What I am suggesting Dave, is that you probably have a false impression of what your retirement will or could be like, and I don't think this course helped matters."

"I guess so," he replied. "I keep getting mixed messages about what to expect."

I explained that there are two distinct areas of retirement planning covering the financial and the non-financial or lifestyle issues. The financial side, based on an established body of knowledge, which most financial planners are highly trained and accredited to handle. Unfortunately, things are different on the non-financial side. Anyone can claim to be an expert in this field and the body of knowledge on the non-financial side is weak, to say the least.

"I refer to this as the traditional model," I said indicating the seminar outline. "It was developed over forty years ago when retirement and retirees were different from today, but the problem is, it no longer applies. Retirees today, people like you, are a different kettle of fish. Most books and courses, including the one you took, are variations of the traditional model. That's why I told you that I had a problem with this course."

However, the proof is in the pudding. Clearly, the course Dave attended did not help him with his concerns about retirement. In addition, based on my experience, Dave is not alone in this regard. Most people have these same concerns when thinking about life after work.

"OK," I said. "Let me describe what you can expect. I can assure you that it is quite different from this. However, before we start, the sun is starting to get to me. I have been out here for a while and I'm going into the house to get a cold drink. Do you want anything?"

"Sure," said Dave. "Whatever you're having will be fine."

The lifestyle side of retirement education involves many dimensions and issues and given Dave's anxiety, I realized that I had to start at the beginning. I suspected that like many people, he really didn't understand retirement and that his image was probably out of date. It was also apparent that the course he took reinforced this false image. When we resumed painting I pointed out that the first thing he had to do was re-evaluate and update his image of retirement.

"I don't think that's the problem," he replied. "I have a pretty good idea of what retirement is. My problem is, I'm just not sure if I am ready for it."

Dave's problem ran deeper than he realized. It was not simply a matter of not being sure if he was ready for retirement. His problem stemmed in part from the meaning he attached to retirement, and his subsequent action - or in his case lack of action - toward it.

Definition of the Situation

To appreciate Dave's problem and the solution I presented, we can take a brief look at a theory identified as 'Situational Analysis'. Most social scientists base their thinking and research pursuits on established social theory. It provides a framework or vantage point for analysis. My academic interests focused on a group of social psychologists, with a particular affinity for the insights of W.I. Thomas. Writing in the 1920's, Thomas developed a concept called 'the definition of the situation'. For our purposes, he demonstrated that one capacity that differentiates man from animals is that the latter act primarily on instinct, while the former have the ability to examine and deliberate before acting. He referred to the act of examination and deliberation as a stage that preceded action. We pause, and consciously or subconsciously, try to make sense of a situation. Based on our interpretation, or the meaning we attach to that situation (our definition of the situation), we act accordingly. Thomas succinctly presented this insight in a single sentence: "If men define situations as real, they are real in their consequences."(1)

In other words, people respond not only to the objective features of the situation, but also, and often mainly, to the meaning that the situation has for them. This explains why two people faced with the same situation might react to it in totally different ways. If one person sees a glass as half-full, while another sees the same glass as half-empty, we have two different definitions of the same situation (viewing a glass of water). Alternatively, if two people attend a movie, one enjoys it, and the other doesn't, again we have different definitions of that situation, and two potentially different ways of reacting to that situation. If a movie critic saw the same movie, he or she would define it differently and likely approach and react to the movie in an entirely different way. Looking upon retirement as a situation defined differently by different people, one would expect different meanings of, reactions to, and ways to approach retirement.

Getting back to Dave's problem of mixed feelings and uncertainty about retirement, to my mind he had two problems. The first was that his definition of the situation (his pending retirement) did not reflect reality. He did not base it on personal experiences, but on observing the experiences of other retirees, the media, images of retirement in the past, and hearsay. Unfortunately, the course he attended exacerbated his false image of retirement (that's why I told him that I was troubled by the course). His other problem was that he lacked the tools to help him make the transition from work to retirement. Because no one can experience retirement in advance, there is no reason to assume that one can make the transition without proper guidelines.

My plan was to present him a few facts that might help him redefine retirement so that it more accurately reflected reality. I also planned to teach him the tools I developed to help ensure that his retirement would be worthwhile and enjoyable. By clarifying his definition of his pending retirement, and by providing him with the tools for the transition to retirement, he would be on his way to solving his dilemma.

The Jack Story

To underscore how our definition of a situation can influence behavior, I recall a joke that I call the Jack Story. It's an old joke but I think the message is clear.

A salesman was driving home from a successful sales trip thinking about his loving wife and children who would greet him when he arrived just in time for dinner. Suddenly, BANG, he had a flat tire. His first impression was, "now I'll be late for dinner." As he got out of his car, he thought to himself, "Why am I worrying? So, I'll be a little late. I made good money this trip; I'll fix the tire and be on my way." When he opened his trunk, he discovered the jack was missing. Again he thought, "There is no point in getting upset. I passed a gas station a while ago, it's a beautiful day, so I'll walk to the gas station, get a jack, and be on my way." After walking a few miles he thought to himself, "I am in the middle of nowhere; for sure the guy will charge me for the jack. Well, it can't be too much. Anyway, I had a very successful trip, so it doesn't matter." As he continued to ponder his predicament, he started to worry - "I am at his mercy he could charge me anything he wants. I don't have any other options; he can really take advantage of me." As he got closer to the gas station, he got madder and madder expecting to be overcharged for the jack. Finally, he reached the gas station; the attendant approached with a smile and said, "Yes sir, can I help you?" The salesman was so angry, he yelled back...

After telling him the Jack Story, I said, "The point is, because he convinced himself that he would be overcharged for the jack, he got so angry that he no longer wanted it. To apply this to retirement, if a person's image of retirement is negative, if they expect it to be empty and meaningless, they might end up thinking,

KEEP YOUR !@}#?% RETIREMENT! I DON'T WANT IT ANYWAY.

And if they think that way, their retirement may turn out that way."

"It's only negative because I am confused about what I should do," said Dave.

"I realize that," I said. "But to help overcome your confusion first you have to clarify your image of retirement."

"If you insist," he said as though to humor me. "Start clarifying."

"First," I explained, "I have a confession to make."

He paused, placed his paintbrush on the edge of the can, sat down on his stool and said, "Start confessing, my son."

I continued to paint and said, "I have been involved in retirement education for more than twenty years, and my confession is that I hate the word retirement."

"You hate it," he exclaimed. He picked up his brush and started to paint. Obviously, my confession wasn't as exciting as he hoped it would be.

"The problem," I said, "lies not with the word itself, but with a history of bad press and with the false and negative images the word can conjure up."

"What do you mean?" he asked.

To explain what I meant I asked him a simple question. I asked him to define retirement.

He thought about this, painted a few strokes on my fence, and said, "Well I suppose it means giving up your job; ending your career."

"Yes and no," I replied.

"What do you mean by that?" he asked.

"Well on the one hand your definition reflects the general image most people have of retirement. Even the dictionary defines retirement as withdrawal from active working life. Nevertheless, I disagree with the definition. Think about it, Dave. A definition should describe an entity. Your definition refers to what you are giving up. It doesn't describe, explain, or give us any idea of what retirement is. It's like defining day as not night, or leisure as not work. Besides, if you define retirement as giving up work, then we have a problem with people who ease into retirement, or retire and then go back to work. Are they retired, or not?"

"They are semi-retired," he replied.

"So they are half or partially retired?" I said somewhat facetiously. "My point is, defining retirement as giving up work is the traditional image that no longer applies. As we discussed this before, this image focused on what people gave up, rather than on what they gained."

"Do you have a better definition?" he asked.

"I think so," I replied. "But first let me ask you another question. Besides giving up work, what other meanings do we apply to the 'R' word?"

The 'R' word?" he replied inquisitively.

"That's how I refer to the word 'retire' because of all the negative baggage it carries," I said.

To help him with the answer I continue, "For instance in baseball when a batter strikes out, we say he retired the batter. Can you think of any other ways we use the 'R' word?"

He thought about this for a moment and said, "I know, to go to sleep."

That's a good one," I said. "We also use retire to refer to retreating, or to withdraw or take out of circulation. In addition, we refer to a shy or modest person as retiring. Are you beginning to see the problem?"

"I never thought about it that way," he replied.

All these meanings point in one direction - withdrawal. Of course, there is nothing wrong with retiring a debt, or going to sleep if you are tired. The problem is, when referring to giving up work, business or a career, the "R" word implicitly reflects advanced age and the other negative uses of the word. It reflects an image of retirement that prevailed in the past. One or two generations ago, the image of retirement saw people leaving work at age 65. They received a gold watch, the lucky ones received a pension, most did not lead a particularly fulfilling or lengthy life in retirement, and most did not expect much from retirement. We have only to think of our grandparents or in some cases, our parents to evoke an image of retirement that we hope will not apply to us. In the past, expressions such as *over the hill* (perpetuated by greeting card companies) along with a little help from the media, reinforced this negative image of retirement. The problem is, the implicit negative meanings hidden in the "R" word are inappropriate and out of step with the new retirement.

Today we are on the verge of a major upheaval. The Baby Boomers born between 1946 and 1965 are starting to retire and they face a set of life circumstances that are significantly different from those faced by their counterpart in the past. They are richer, will live longer, are more highly educated, expect more from retirement, and account for 56 percent of the adult population. Given these differences, the negativity that accompanies the 'R' word is simply out of step with a new generation of Boomer retirees.

Finding a neutral term to replace the "R" word can be a challenge. Marketing and advertising specialists are particularly perplexed with this problem. They realize the enormity of this market, but must tread softly to avoid alienating its members. Admittedly, we are only dealing with a name. Nevertheless, often the meaning behind a name can have far-reaching effects.

"There is another use of the 'R' word that really bothers me," I said.

When I conduct group seminars and workshops, I use overheads to highlight certain crucial points. I stood there with my paintbrush in hand wondering how I could replicate an overhead slide. The solution was obvious. I dipped my paintbrush in the paint can and wrote on the fence.

To me, a blatant misuse of the "R" word is a Retirement Home. I can recall when a Retirement Home used to be called an Old Folks or a Senior's Home. It seems that these terms are no longer politically correct so marketing experts have re-packaged a Senior's Home as a Retirement Home. The service and clientele are the same, only the name has changed. Clearly, we have a problem when homes for the aged are called homes for the retired. This innocent marketing strategy reinforces the negative image of retirement as retreat or withdrawal as well as the connection with aging. A retirement home has absolutely nothing to do with retirement.

After I painted the image, Dave smiled. He knew what I was getting at.

"Is it a home for retirees? I asked. "If so, I don't think either one of us will be ready to retire for a very long time."

"The problem with the 'R' word," I continued, "is that retirement has had its share of bad press in the past and most people don't stop to think about how that can affect their view of retirement. If you think of retirement as giving up work, retreat, withdrawal, or going to sleep, and if you see a connection to growing old, clearly you do not have much to look forward to. It can become a self-fulfilling prophecy.

"The good news, Dave, is just because these negative characteristics applied to retirement in the past, there is no reason to assume that they apply to retirement or retirees today."

"Take a look at your friends," I said. "These are future retirees. It should be obvious that they will not withdraw or follow the old pattern when they retire. Perhaps now you can understand why I hate the 'R' Word. It is simply out of step with reality."

"I never thought of it that way," he replied. "It's true. I remember greeting cards about retirement that joked about it being the end of the line. I don't know if they have these kinds of cards anymore."

"I don't think so," I said. "The card companies probably realized that people weren't buying these negative cards anymore. But we are still left with the problem of the 'R' word, so I will show you how we can re-define retirement so that it will be more compatible with retirement today."

A New Frame of Reference

When I started conducting retirement education workshops, I recognized the problem with the 'R' word and one of my first concerns was to update the image and definition of retirement. I wanted to come up with a new word that would be instantly recognizable, effective, and that would clearly delineate what retirement is, not what it isn't. The word had to reflect the positive nature of retirement, and it could not refer to age because age has nothing to do with retirement. So words such as senior, mature, elderly, or golden age (that's why I cringed when Dave told me that the seminar leader referred to retirement as the golden years), were out of the question. Eventually I came up with a replacement for the 'R' word.

I painted the word "RETIRE" on my fence. Then I said, "One positive thing about the 'R' word is it is instantly recognizable. So for its replacement, we start with the 'R' word and add a dash." I added the dash.

"What image comes to mind now?" I asked.

He smiled and said, "Getting new tires for your car."

"Exactly. The word re-tire with a dash suggests getting new tires or a 'new set of wheels'. When was the last time you bought new tires?" I asked.

"Believe it or not," said Dave, "we visited our son a few weeks ago and I bought new tires before we left."

"So, how did you feel after getting new tires?"

"Well, I suppose it felt good. The tires looked good and I definitely felt good about the safety factor."

"When you get a new set of wheels you feel great, you can go anywhere - around town, across the country - feeling confident that the journey will be safe and comfortable. Let it rain, let it snow, I don't care, I have new tires on my car. Tire manufacturers love this image - it helps sell tires.

"Now transfer this image to your re-tirement," I explained. "To re-tire with a dash is like getting a new set of wheels for your life. It can involve rejuvenation, you can go anywhere, do anything, and it allows for new opportunities, you can please yourself.

"Adding a dash also refers to mixing in something different to improve the original like adding a dash of salt or humor. This is precisely what re-tire with a dash involves. We are adding something different, or spicing up an outdated image of retirement."

This new description characterizes what the new Boomer re-tirees hope to gain from re-tirement. It implies preparation for a journey, movement, action, rejuvenation, freedom, and a fresh new start. In contrast to 'retire' (without the dash), which implies withdrawal, retreat or going to sleep, 're-tire' implies a new beginning.

"From now on Dave, whenever you see or think of the 'R' word, spice it up, mentally add the dash. Think of getting a new set of wheels to embark on a new life journey. It can be anything you want and the best time to begin this journey is following a work career. When the time comes for you to say, 'I am re-tired', say it with pride."

For our purposes, to re-tire (with the dash) refers to preparing for a new life journey. When you re-tire you are gaining something (a new lease on life). When you retire (without the dash), you are giving up something (work, your turn at bat, life). In fact, the only positive uses of the word retire is in reference to going to sleep, and paying off a loan. Moreover, because re-tirement does not refer to giving up work, it is possible to re-tire to a new line of work.

NOTE: From this point on, *re-tire* refers to the process of preparing for a fresh new journey and the best time to begin this journey is following a work or business career. It also refers to the act of rejuvenating your life. *Re-tiree* and *re-tired* refer to the rejuvenated individual who is taking the journey, and *re-tirement* refers to the time during which the journey takes place. The word *retirement* (without the hyphen) will refer to the old traditional use of the term as applied to generations of retirees in the past. You will also see it used in direct quotes from your re-tirement mentors.

"I like this new way of looking at re-tirement," said Dave.

"Then I think you will like my definition," I replied as I painted the following words on the fence."

"Re-tire with a dash is defined as a career earned from and following work."

"The key here," I continued, "is to think of re-tirement as a career. I am not suggesting that you will work in re-tirement, although many people do. What I am suggesting is that like most work careers, your re-tirement career will develop and evolve over time. In addition, by emphasizing that you earned re-tirement, we are acknowledging its worth as a reward following work. It is something to be proud of. You have earned it."

Viewed this way, we are accurately describing the new re-tirement. It is positive, dynamic, progressive, and does not refer to age. This new concept does not carry any excess or negative baggage, and because it makes no reference to giving up work, this eliminates the need for awkward phrases like 'semi-retired' when a re-tiree returns to work."

Life Career

I went on to explain how a re-tirement career emerges as the fusion of the individual's work and leisure career. To start, I painted a line on my fence to represent a work career and said, "Imagine that this line represents all the jobs that most people hold during their work career. I realize that dentistry is different in that it usually follows a distinct career path, but most people start their first job and this leads to something else, which leads to something else, and so on. Moreover, when they reach the end of their work career, often they end up doing something that may be completely different from when they started their work career.

"The same is likely to happen with your re-tirement career," I replied. "It will develop and evolve and what you end up doing may be quite different from what you have in mind now."

"I hope so," he replied, "because I have nothing in mind now."

Re-tirement as a career is an important characteristic of the new re-tirement. Retirement without the dash suggested an implicit emphasis on retreat and referred to an event, the day after the last day of work, or as a life stage. The new re-tirement is more dynamic. It is a career that will develop and progress over time.

Obviously, there are major differences between a work and re-tirement career. The need for income and security guide most work careers, while the desire to enjoy oneself will guide a re-tirement career. I am not suggesting that job satisfaction does not influence a working career. However, let's face it, the bottom line is to earn a living and feel secure. If the opportunity to make more money or increase job security came along, most people would probably make the career move. Another difference between a work career and a re-tirement career relates to the amount of control a person has over how each will progress.

Most people fall into their first job based on various circumstances, like having worked there in the summer. For others perhaps a friend or relative worked there, it may have been the first job offered, it paid more, or a certain Personnel Director decided to hire you. Having started that first job, your life took a certain direction. If you changed jobs, it is likely that circumstance also influenced the new job partially. If you look back on your work career, you can probably see how many small circumstances along with the decisions of others have influenced where you are now. Suppose your first job was with a different company. It is possible that your life may have turned out to be quite different. Circumstance and the decisions of others exert a strong influence on the development of a working career.

"The main benefit of your re-tirement career, Dave, is that you are the boss. You have the freedom to take charge and guide your life so it will be worthwhile and enjoyable. There will be uncertainties but they will be minimal. The beauty of re-tirement is that if you ever feel that something is missing, that you are not enjoying life to the fullest, you have the freedom to make adjustments. Most people do not have this freedom in their working career."

"That's certainly true," he said. "But sometimes having all that freedom, or free time, can be a problem."

"Absolutely," I replied. "And that is what Life Goal Planning is all about. But let's take this one step a time."

Next, I introduced Dave to another career represented by a line parallel to the work career line, and said, "If you think about it, your leisure can also be viewed as a career. Like your work career, it has and will continue to develop and evolve. However, a major characteristic of your leisure career is that it is highly influenced by your work career. As circumstances change in your work career, you may see parallel changes in your leisure career. An obvious example is if somebody receives a promotion to a more senior position and makes more money, it is likely that their leisure choices may reflect this difference. On the other hand, we may choose some activities to compensate for our work, or we may choose others as an extension of our work, such as playing golf with a client or friends from work. And sometimes there will be no relationship between the two."

To complete the image of a Life Career I included the re-tirement career. "Your re-tirement career is an extension of your work and leisure careers. Together they comprise your Life Career. Your re-tirement career will develop and evolve as the fusion of your work and leisure careers. It is the best of both."

"Re-tirement is the opportunity to do something worthwhile as with work, with the pleasure of enjoyment as in leisure. You no longer have to do what others expect of you, but what you freely undertake on your own. Job and family responsibilities are behind you and you can draw on a wealth of experiences, insights, and realistic aspirations. It is a new career based on the coming together or amalgamation of your previous work and leisure careers. In some cases, especially for women who traditionally live longer than men, a re-tirement career can be longer than a work career."

"It all sounds very good," said Dave. "But I still have no idea of what I can do when I re-tire."

"That's understandable," I replied, "especially since the seminar you took gave you the wrong impression of what re-tirement is all about."

The sun continued to beat down and Dave offered to get us another drink. He was gone a long time and I initially thought that he had enough painting for one day. However, when he returned he brought sandwiches. It seemed that his definition of his re-tirement situation was beginning to change and he was willing to learn more. It also seemed that he was willing to continue painting my fence. Tom Sawyer would have been proud of me.

Life Goal Planning

We ate in the shade and it was clear that Dave could use a little more help than was possible through our backyard chat. I told him that after working with pre-re-tirees for many years, I developed a process I called Life Goal Planning and it was designed for people in his situation and once he understood how it worked, he would have the tools to create a re-tirement that would be worthwhile and enjoyable. I indicated that we didn't have time today to go through the process and painting my fence wasn't exactly the ideal learning environment. I suggested that we could meet again to go through the process but that we could cover some other areas to give him greater insight or clues into the new re-tirement with a dash. He liked the idea of meeting again, and I liked the idea of having him continue to paint my fence.

When we resumed painting, I said, "You have to remember, Dave, there are two forms of spending in re-tirement. You will be spending time and money and the problem is, when most people prepare for re-tirement, they think mainly about the money side - financial planning. Of course money is very important, but don't underestimate the significance of how you spend your time on re-tirement happiness."

"But the two are related," said Dave. "It costs money to spend time, you know what I mean."

"I know exactly what you mean," I replied. "I agree that they are related. I am suggesting that because there are two forms of spending in re-tirement, there should be two forms of planning for re-tirement. You should not leave up to chance, your planning for how you will spend your time. In addition, because financial planning is based on having a financial goal, which in turn is based on knowing how you will spend your time, the two forms of planning complement each other and that is what Life Goal Planning is all about."

"Obviously not everyone has this problem," I added. "I have met many people who can hardly wait to re-tire because they have a million things they want to do. But I have run hundreds of pre-re-tirement workshops and in my experience close to seventy percent of pre-re-tirees do not have concrete plans for re-tirement."

"I know," said Dave. "That's what frustrates me. I know I have this great opportunity, but I just don't what to jump into it quite yet. I just don't know what I will do with myself when I re-tire."

Advice From Your Re-tirement Mentors

There are several reasons why Life Goal Planning can benefit you in re-tirement, but the main reason is when asked what advice they would give to other dentists who are contemplating re-tirement, next to planning your finances, the most frequently mentioned recommendation was to plan your time and remain active.

This suggestion cuts to the chase - it's the bottom line. They are speaking from experience and had the opportunity to summarize their feelings about re-tirement in a single statement. I recommend that you heed their advice. Here is a summary of their responses followed by a few examples.

Table 1-1. Advice From Your Re-tirement Mentors

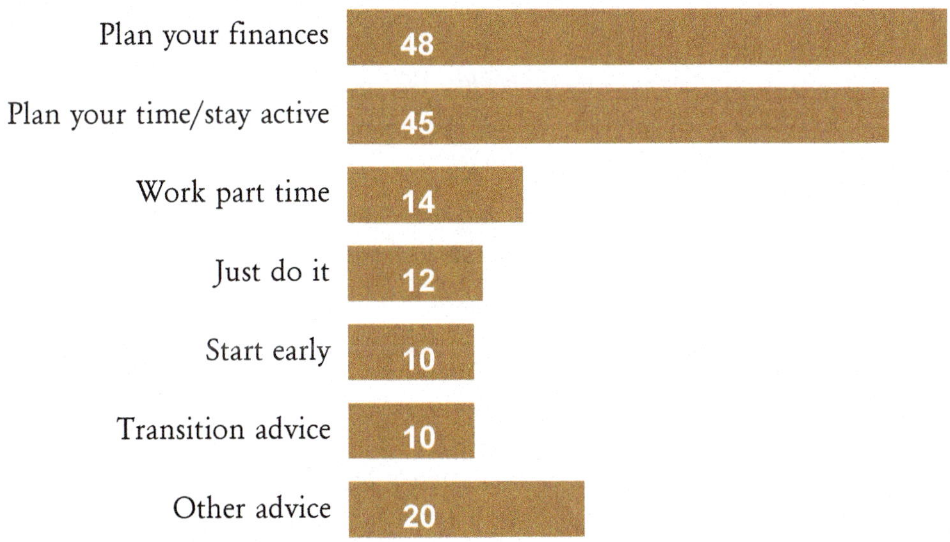

*Other advice included considerations for your spouse or family, and seeking help from retired colleagues or professional planners.

Plan Your Time

It should not come as a surprise that your re-tirement mentors encourage you to plan how you will spend your time in re-tirement. In some cases, the reference was very general, such as "*Be sure to have enough outside interests to keep you busy*", to specific recommendations such as, H*ave a life outside of dentistry. Develop hobbies, interests... For me learning to play a musical instrument was the smartest thing.*" When you learn how to apply the Life Goal Planning techniques, you will be well on your way to having a plan.

I would recommend that dentists plan for a future that would include something to give meaning and purpose to their time. Include in that plan something other than dentistry. I always planned to do volunteer dentistry in retirement, yet due to a disability I am unable to practice clinical dentistry.

Make sure that you have a variety of interests that you want to pursue. You need to have some things to replace the stimulation of practicing dentistry.

Plan ahead, start now doing hobbies that interest you and you can get more involved in during retirement. Set it up so you can do what you want when you want and don't sit around idle.

Planning or finding a purpose, activities and comaraderie prior to retiring is as important, if not more important, than financial planning.

Please find a new passion. I know, we as dentists, are very driven and passionate about our profession. If you don't find a substitute for that you will feel lost.

The advice is different depending on what age one is retiring at. If one is retiring at age 65 to 70 the advice might be more along the lines of 'find a hobby' or 'start traveling. As for someone like me who decided to retire at age 61 my goal or mission was to find another purpose or passion.

Think clearly and for many months about this life changing decision. have a clear path on what you will be doing each day, After a few months being home or free gets old and can become boring and lonely.

Make sure you know what you will do with your time in retirement. If you do not have a clue how you will spend your days and you still like what you doing don't retire. If you have a high standard of living make sure you can cut that back and still be happy and have things to do.

Plan Your Finances

Next to planning your time, 48% strongly encouraged you to plan your finances - the earlier the better. Although Life After Dentistry does not deal directly with financial planning, you will learn how Life Goal Planning can actually enhance your financial plan. Here are a few comments from your re-tirement mentors.

Get out of debt as soon as you can and invest in your retirement as early as you can...Social Security is a poor investment with little return. Don't count on Social Security to be of much help when you retire.

Plan for at least 2-3 years, do not think that you will receive a financial windfall from the sale of the practice, make sure your finances are secure, be aware that it is not your practice anymore, and many associate agreements end in mutual discord...experiment with how a retirement day might work after 6 months of not working.

It's never too early to start serious planning. Learn to be the expert who oversees your advisers (nobody loves and understands you and your money like you do).

Be prepared financially. I think if you have enough money to retire everything else seems to fall into place. Start saving from the first - -don't wait till the end of your career or you probably won't be able to retire with confidence and less stress.

Get life insurance, health insurance, will, etc. in place. Work with a reputable financial planner. Discuss plan carefully with spouse.

Plan financially to put 10% of your income away for retirement from the second year of working, no later than the fifth year.

Save from day one. Treat your savings as a bill that needs to be paid each and every month. Fully half of your retirement savings will come from what you save in your first 10 years in practice. Don't make any stupid investments, and don't invest in things you don't know. Do your homework so you know what your advisors are doing for (not to) you.

Work Part-time

If you are in good health, work part time a bit longer than you had originally planned or thought about. But above all make sure you are well prepared financially. Living to 100 yrs is possible and it can tax your plans.

On my favorite coffee mug is a perfect saying: Do what you like, like what you do. I have been most fortunate to be able to remain active in dentistry. I still enjoy the profession. By cutting my hours, I have so far been able to keep away from burn out. At 57, I am cutting down my hours significantly giving me time to enjoy with family at home while keeping adequate income stream. At present, I would like to keep my nose in the office a few days a week till I am 68.

If you are in good health and still love dentistry and interacting with staff, and patients, you might consider working part time or volunteering at a free health dental clinic.

DO NOT RETIRE TOO SOON!!! If you enjoy what you do - slow it down but DO NOT walk away cold. If you have good health and skills - continue to serve others.

Just Do It/Enjoy Yourself

Several people referred to what I call the 'Nike Approach' - just do it! Others offered more philosophical advice; encouraging you to enjoy yourself in re-tirement.

When you feel it's right, just do it. Don't listen to the financial pundits that say work hard and build to the last moment so the practice value is worth more. It's about patient care (not financial satisfaction) It is often too much about money!

Plan for it and enjoy it. Do not believe you must die at the chair.

Just do it when it's the right time. Only you can know the right time. You may screw up, but that's how it is.

Don't wait to long to retire do it when you can enjoy the world. Life is to short.

Do it soon, but stay involved. give back there is a lot of need out there.

Transition Advice

Some people gave specific advice referring to the transition to re-tirement. For example,

Really find an associate with the same values and try your hardest to make them successful. Then they will want you still to contribute and still be part of the practice. The staff will love the nice transition and you can work as much or little as you want.

Make sure you are financially secure. Have a transition plan in place so you can leave your patients in good hands when you are gone. Announce your retirement plans to your staff and patients at least six months before your retirement date so you and your patients have the opportunity to say 'Good-bye' to each other.

Make sure your transition of the practice is a good one. I sold to a corporate entity and that made it very easy and smooth. Plus I got more for my practice than the brokers were willing to do.

Consider an associate 2 or more years before you plan to retire.

Other Advice

Several people gave advice that did not fit into any of the above categories but that are worthy of your consideration.

Take the time to plan. Make sure your spouse/significant other is on board with your decision and understands the implications on his/her life as well as yours.

Take care of your health - nothing is as important as this - NOTHING. Get your financial world in order early. Taper off your commitments to the office gradually - -think about volunteering to the under served - you have a skill set that is in big time demand

Retire when you do not yet have to. It is a very good feeling to put up the drill when you are at the top of your game.

I found it hard to live in same community with past patients, always asking for dental advice and about treatment option.

Too late now to change much. Try to get a good balance in the years you may have left. You will never have enough money, but your future is a lot shorter. Enjoy Every Day!

The message is clear. Money alone cannot guarantee happiness in re-tirement. How you spend your time, can be the most important element that contributes to re-tirement happiness. To emphasize this point I asked Dave if he knew of anyone who was well off financially and was not enjoying re-tirement.

"I sure do," he replied. "You've just described my brother-in-law. He retired a few years ago and was having some real problems. Money-wise he was OK, but he used to be a high-powered executive and my sister kept complaining about him hanging around the house all the time. Eventually he settled down. However, he went through some rough times. I suppose my friend Les is in this situation, and if something doesn't happen soon, I'm going to be in that situation."

"On the other hand," I said, "through my research and workshop experience I have met people who were living below the poverty line and who said that re-tirement was the best time of their life. Clearly, re-tirement happiness involves more than money. The reason my program is called a Life Goal Planning is because re-tirement today, the new re-tirement, in many ways involves uncharted territory. First, as I explained, the old traditional approach to lifestyle planning is out of date. Therefore, we definitely need a new set of directions for re-tirement happiness that focuses on how you will spend your time. Second, each person's re-tirement is unique. You can look at other people, read about it, or attend seminars, but your experience will be unique. Just because your friend Les is having problems, it doesn't mean that you will have problems. Because of this, you could use some guidance. The third reason is you cannot truly understand what re-tirement will be like until you experience it. There are no dress rehearsals so a proven method will help guide you."

"If I don't know what it will be like until I re-tire, how can you help me?" he asked.

"That's a good question," I replied. "But do me a favor and let's come back to this question after you learn about Life Goal Planning, then you will be able to answer the question yourself."

"Ok," he replied.

"As I said, re-tirement is unique because there are no dress rehearsals. When we experience other life changes, we usually have a good idea of what it will be like in advance. For most people when they started working full-time, it does not come as a complete surprise. Why? Because we had some experience in this area by going to school. We learned about punctuality, competing with others, and so on, before we started to work full-time. In addition, many people have part-time jobs in the summer. So they have a good idea of what working full time would be like before they finished school. However, re-tirement is different. You can't experience it in advance.

Most people have not had much experience with extended periods of free time. When you were at school, you had summer vacation and when you joined the world of work you probably had a few weeks vacation each year. Nevertheless, re-tirement is different. It's not like a vacation. Time can be your greatest ally or nemesis. The questions you will have to face include: Will your gains outweigh your losses? How are you going to use your new freedom? Will you use it to replace the satisfactions lost from work, to help you grow in a way that is satisfying or fulfilling, or will you rely on the vague hope that life will somehow take care of itself? In all likelihood, you could use a little help.

Before introducing Life Goal Planning, I wanted to clarify a few issues that many people associate with re-tirement, but that on a closer look can actually inhibit re-tirement happiness. The first is the misplaced notion of confusing re-tirement with aging. I present this in more detail in Chapter 7.

"Dave, I recall when we talked about the retirement (without the dash) seminar you attended, the course included several subjects that related to health and aging such as medicine, keeping fit, and safety at home. Did the speaker really cover safety at home and medicine?"

"We didn't spend a lot of time on this, but I recall that they did mention them."

"First of all, given that re-tirement is a career earned from and following work, what does safety at home or medicine, have to do with re-tirement?"

Dave thought about this and replied, "If you put it that way, absolutely nothing."

"OK," I went on, "What do keeping fit, nutrition, and health have to do with re-tirement?"

"Everything," he replied. "If you're not in good health how can you enjoy your re-tirement?"

I could see I had my work cut out for me. This argument is common and it underlies a misconception that requires clarification. I decided to apply some logic.

"I agree that health is important, but would you agree, Dave, that keeping fit, nutrition, and good health are important and could affect enjoyment while you are working?"

"Of course they could," he replied.

"What about when you were younger, like when you were at school, were they important then?"

"Health is always important," said Dave.

"OK, so we agree. Health is always important, not just at re-tirement."

"For sure," he quickly responded.

"Have you ever attended a course on, say time management?"

"As a matter of fact I have," he replied.

"Did you ever discuss keeping fit, health, or nutrition in this course?"

Dave looked at me as though I was crazy. "Of course not," he replied.

"Why not? Isn't health important for managing your time?" I fired back.

"I suppose so, but it's a separate issue."

"Well if health is important at all stages in life, not just re-tirement, and if it is a separate issue for a work related course, why should it be part of re-tirement planning? Remember, we are talking about changing from a work to a re-tirement career."

"Because we are getting older and eventually our health may become a problem," said Dave.

"So it's not a health or a re-tirement issue, but an age concern," I replied.

"I guess so," he replied.

"So we agree that a lecture on health does not belong in a course on re-tirement."

"If you put it that way, I guess not," he replied with a smile.

"How were health and fitness handled at the workshop? Did they bring in a speaker?"

"Yes, I think she was a nutritionist."

"Now be honest Dave. After hearing her presentation, did you change your eating or exercise habits?"

A slight smile came to Dave's face and he said, "Pass the beer and pretzels, I just ran out."

He didn't have to respond. People know what they should and should not eat or how much exercise they should do, and a speaker, no matter how well intentioned, is not likely to change things - certainly not in the long run. In fact, I maintain that a speaker on health can be a detriment in a re-tirement education program.

I reminded him of two things we agreed on. First, that health is not a re-tirement issue, and second, that he did not change his eating or exercise habits after the nutrition lecture. It follows, therefore, that the only thing the health lecture accomplished was to reinforce the false assumption that when people re-tire there is a likelihood that they are going to be sick or are getting old. If not, why include it?

"The main problem," I said, "is if you believe there is a connection between re-tirement and poor health or old age it could become a self-fulfilling prophecy. You could believe it to the point that you may create a problem. If you view retirement the old traditional way as withdrawal, putting out of commission, going to sleep, and so on, you can see why some retirement books or courses include a discussion on health. But if you view re-tirement as changing careers, health becomes a separate issue."

"I think I see what you are getting at," he said.

I pointed out that re-tirement is not a disease and it never has, nor ever will, kill anyone. If a person is despondent, bored, lonely, or inactive, these can have a negative effect on health and longevity. I am not denying this fact. These conditions, however, are not exclusive to re-tirement. They can occur at any stage in life.

I continued, "The problem is, some writers and seminar leaders who discuss exercise or eating habits leave the impression that re-tirement can be bad for your health. Nothing can be further from the truth. As I see it, the only connection between re-tirement, health, and exercise is you will no longer be able to use the classic 'I don't have enough time' excuse. Re-tirement gives you the opportunity to plan your own time."

Once Dave realized that aging and health were not re-tirement issues, we were making significant progress in clarifying his definition of his re-tirement situation.

To identify another potential problem, I said, "I see they also covered retirement activities such as," I read him the list, "Travel, leisure, hobbies, volunteering, and second careers. In addition, here's an interesting topic, sex after 60. I suppose sex could be classified as a re-tirement activity."

"I hope so," said Dave.

"I hate to disappoint you," I said. "But sex is not a re-tirement activity."

"What?" he replied acting surprised. "That does it. I've made up my mind. I'm never going to re-tire."

"Seriously, Dave," I said. "So, people have sex after 60. What does that have to do with re-tirement? Perhaps if they called it sex after giving up work, then it would at least sound relevant to retirement without the dash. By calling it sex after 60, they are referring to age, not to re-tirement. Like health and aging, sex is a separate issue that has nothing to do with the transition to your re-tirement career. You may have learned something in the workshop, but you have to admit, sex is a totally inappropriate topic in a re-tirement course."

"If you insist," said Dave. "It may not be relevant but it sure would spice up your workshop."

"I'll keep that in mind," I said. "And I'll call you in as an expert speaker."

Glancing at the course outline once again I said, "I see the course included a section on managing stress. Clearly, the person who designed this course regards retirement as stressful. If that's the case, I think you would be wise never to re-tire. No wonder you have mixed feelings, Dave."

My favorite example of an irrelevant and inappropriate retirement topic is a discussion on funerals. I came across this issue in a book on retirement and it is clear how the author views retirement and the type of negative message this sends to the reader.

Another issue that can create problems is the common assumption that re-tirement is similar to leisure. Referring once again to the retirement course outline, I asked Dave how they presented this issue.

"I can't remember all the details," he answered. "But I remember him saying that retirement was like leisure earned from a lifetime of work. He also talked about taking a leisure interest and somehow working it into your re-tirement. I suppose that means I will be spending my re-tirement painting fences."

"If we don't finish soon, that may be the case," I agreed.

After refilling Dave's paint bucket, I said, "Actually, Dave, I wanted to talk about this because many people think about re-tirement as similar to leisure, and this is not necessarily the case. I agree that you earn re-tirement from work, but I do not agree that it is leisure. If you recall our discussion on life careers, I pointed out that your re-tirement career involved a fusion of your work and leisure careers."

To explain this distinction I asked him to define leisure. He thought about it for a minute and said, "I suppose it's doing something unstructured, outside work, doing something in your free time."

"That's a good definition," I replied. "And we use the term leisurely to refer to doing something without haste. So my next question is, if leisure is free time or doing something slowly, would you say that this is an accurate description of re-tirement?"

"Well it's free time," he replied. "But I hope it won't be too leisurely."

"So we agree. Our definition of leisure does not suit re-tirement. Besides, earlier you agreed that re-tirement was a career earned from and following work."

"Yes," he said.

"Another problem is that sometimes we think of leisure as secondary or trivial pursuits. However, re-tirement is a 'non-trivial pursuit'. Clearly they are not one and the same."

While teaching at the university, I undertook a major research project looking at perceptions of work and leisure among retirees. When we asked whether they viewed re-tirement as leisure, in most cases they did not view it that way. When asked how they defined work and leisure, we found an interesting distinction between pre and post-re-tirees. Before people re-tire, they tend to look on leisure as free time (similar to Dave's definition). However, after they re-tire, because most of their time is free time, they differentiated between work and leisure activities based on degrees of enjoyment. They defined leisure as enjoyable activities, and work as not-so-enjoyable activities.

This brings us to a common problem among some re-tirees who think they can take a former leisure interest, increase the time spent on that interest, and that it will be as much fun or as meaningful during re-tirement. Travel is a good example here. While we are working, travel generally derives its meaning in contrast to our everyday life and work. The novelty and excitement of travel can soon wear off, however, if that is all there is to your life. This is not to suggest that not all leisure interests will serve the same purpose in re-tirement, or that travel will not be enjoyable when one re-tires. The point is, many leisure interests derive their meaning in contrast to work, and if work is gone, the leisure interest can similarly lose its meaning. As stated earlier, re-tirement is a career that will develop and evolve as the fusion of your work and leisure careers. It is the best of both and the opportunity to do something worthwhile as with work, with the pleasure of enjoyment as in leisure.

It was time to give Dave a few more clues about what he could expect in re-tirement, so again I turned to the fence.

Looking somewhat perplexed, he asked, "What does that mean?"

I explained that it stands for Central Life Focus. This concept originally applied to work, and it implies that work is a dominant sphere in our life. The type of work we do, our level within the workplace, exerts considerable influence on many other aspects of our life. It can influence our way of thinking and lifestyle and demands a significant portion of our time and energy. For instance, our involvement in the workplace determines how much money we will have to spend, the goodies we can buy, the type of friends we will choose, our leisure interests, and how we will spend our time and money in re-tirement. It determines where we will live, and may even influence whom we will choose as a spouse. As discussed earlier, our leisure career parallels our work career and the latter influences the former.

"When you give up work," I said, "by default, re-tirement will become your Central Life Focus. I am not suggesting that you will have a problem replacing your CLF in re-tirement. All I am saying is that the difference between work and re-tirement as a CLF is that work generally involves one activity, while re-tirement may end up being comprised of several activities. In addition, many of your lifestyle choices formed during your work and leisure careers will carry over to your re-tirement career. Again, I am generalizing, but often we get used to having a single CLF and some people need a dominant CLF in re-tirement. Others can quite happily spread their involvement over several activities."

"For some people, a leisure activity can become a Central Life Focus, but for most people it is not enough to simply spend more time in a leisure activity. I am not suggesting that a leisure interest will not be enjoyable or serve the same purpose in re-tirement. I am simply pointing out that many leisure interests derive their meaning in contrast to work, and if work is gone the leisure interest can similarly lose its meaning or is not sufficient to replace a CLF."

"But I know somebody who contradicts what you are saying," said Dave. "I have a friend who loves to golf and he could hardly wait to re-tire so he could spend all his time golfing. He repairs golf clubs in the winter and is a club marshal. He is totally involved in golf and seems to be quite happy in re-tirement."

"That's a good example," I replied. "But it doesn't totally contradict what I just said. It sounds as though he is not just spending more time playing golf. He expanded his interest through other golf related activities, he started a small business repairing clubs, and presumably as a marshal, he was involved in administrative activities. Together these activities constitute his CLF in re-tirement. I am willing to bet that if he did not expand into other activities and simply played more golf, his re-tirement would not be as fulfilling and he would feel that something was missing from his life."

I asked Dave what he did for leisure and he mentioned playing cards and camping. Using camping as an example, I asked him to explain why he enjoyed camping.

He replied with several reasons that characterized camping and added, "it's a good break from work."

To develop this thought further I said, "Would it be correct to assume that part of the reason you enjoy camping is because it is completely different from your work? For example, it's outdoors, work is indoors; work can be constricting, camping is freely chosen; work is highly structured, camping is the opposite; plus as a bonus, you can camp with whoever you choose."

"Absolutely," replied Dave. "As I said, it is a break from work. Sometimes my job can get quite hectic and camping is total relaxation."

I asked how camping might be different if he was re-tired.

He replied, "Well we might go more often because I would have more time. On the other hand, we might go to different places. Now that you mention it, I suppose it might be a bit different. When Diane and I go camping, the thing we really enjoy is getting away from it all. We may only go for a week or sometimes for a weekend but there is nothing I enjoy more than driving into the country especially when things are going crazy at work. Then again, I like my work and after being away for a few days, I am anxious to get back to it. It's true, if I didn't have work to come back to, camping might not be the same."

"As you can see, your feelings about camping are tied somewhat to your feelings about work. In addition, it is enjoyable partly because it contrasts and is a break from work. At the same time, I wouldn't be surprised if you sometimes thought about work when you are camping. So it is reasonable to expect that your feelings about camping, or any leisure activity for that matter, may be somewhat different when you re-tire."

"Does that mean that I will no longer enjoy camping when I re-tire?" asked Dave.

"Absolutely not," I replied. "It will still be enjoyable but it may not serve the same function in re-tirement. It will take more than camping to replace the satisfaction lost from work. Your golfing friend is a good example of this."

"Another way to think about re-tirement," I continued, "is that it's like winning a mini lottery."

"Yeah, but I worked hard to pay for my re-tirement, whereas a lottery is pure luck."

"But if you think about it, the similarity lies in the fact that your main concerns include making sure your money lasts, and figuring out how you are going to spend your time. Spending time is what Life Goal Planning is all about. By the way, congratulations on your windfall."

"I haven't re-tired yet," said Dave.

"OK, congratulations on your pending windfall."

As an interesting parallel, studies suggest that most lottery winners keep working because often work is more than just about money. According to one study, certainly, money is important, but there are many benefits of work that play a big role: relationships, achievement needs that people have, status needs outside of money[(3)].

We agreed that a break was in order and as we cooled ourselves in the shade, Dave's wife Diane joined us. "You guys have been in the sun too long. How's it going?"

By this point, we had enough even though my fence was not finished.

"I don't know about you," I said, "but I have had enough painting for today and I really have spent too much time in the sun. I want to continue our talk so why not pick up where we left off next weekend?"

"I would like that," said Dave. "I'm still waiting to learn about Life Goal Planning."

"I would be happy to share it with you," I said.

"OK," said Dave looking over at Diane. "We can meet at our house next weekend." He paused for a moment and asked, "Would you mind if we called Les to see if he wants to join us? I think he could really use it."

"By all means," I replied. "That would be a good idea. In fact the process actually works best with a small group."

"Is Les married?" I asked.

"Yes," Diane replied. "I am quite friendly with his wife."

"Then ask her if she wants to join us. That way we will have a small group. In addition, re-tirement is a shared experience and it is best if both partners understand what is going on. Dave, it would be a good idea if you explained to Diane, Les, and his wife some of the things we talked about today - like re-tire with a dash and the new way of viewing re-tirement."

"That's great," said Diane. "We can meet at our house next Sunday."

"Sounds good to me," I said.

"Thanks for your help," said Dave. "I'm starting to feel a little better about re-tirement. I'll call Les and fill them in on what we talked about."

"You're welcome Dave. My fence and I both thank you. Let me know the time and I will be there."

As I headed for the house, I looked back at my fence and realized that I got a little carried away trying to make my point. Perhaps Tom Sawyer wouldn't be so proud of me after all.

Chapter Summary

- The traditional definition of retirement is negatively charged, suggesting withdrawal, retreat, or going to sleep. The main problem is this outdated image can become a self-fulfilling prophecy.
- Retirement is updated as "re-tire" (with a dash) defined as a career earned from and following work.
- To complete the image, a re-tirement career is an extension of your work and leisure careers. It is the best of both and the opportunity to do something worthwhile (as in work) and enjoyable (as in leisure).
- The main advice from our sample of retired dentists was to plan your time, and that is what Life Goal Planning (Part 3) will enable you to do.
- The difference between work and re-tirement as a Central Life Focus is work generally involves one activity, while re-tirement may end up being comprised of several activities.
- Retirement is like winning a (modest) lottery. Your first concern is to make sure your money will last, and because you would not necessarily have to work, you would be concerned with how you would spend your time.

TOP SECRET

2

DO YOU WANT TO KNOW A SECRET?

(The Beatles, 1963)

KEY TO RETIREMENT HAPPINESS

The following Sunday we met at Dave and Diane's house. Les and his wife Janice had arrived before me and after the usual introductions, we sat outside on the patio. Dave had explained to the others most of what he remembered from our conversation last weekend.

To begin I turned to Les and said, "I understand that you are re-tired. That's good; it means you are a professional. We can learn from your experiences."

"I don't think I have much to teach anybody," said Les.

"Don't be so sure," I replied. "As I mentioned to Dave last week, you can't truly understand what re-tirement will be like until you experience it. As a re-tiree, you are an expert so we can learn from your experiences. How long have you been re-tired, Les?"

"About 18 months now," he replied.

"And what are your impressions so far?"

Les looked at Janice, smiled, and said, "I'm not too impressed. I'm enjoying it, but to tell you the truth, at least for me, it's not all that it's cracked up to be."

"What do you mean?" I asked.

"It's hard to explain," said Les. "I'm having a pretty good time but there are times when well, quite frankly, I'm bored. I never thought that would be a problem."

Then Janice said, "Have you heard the expression I married him for better or for worse but not for lunch? Well there is some truth in that."

Dave looked over to me and smiled as if to say 'you've got your work cut out for you.'

"Here's the situation," I said. "Dave and Diane want to learn about re-tirement, and Les and Janice are the experts. By the way, Janice, are you re-tired?"

"I only worked part-time but I stopped when Les re-tired," replied Janice. "I could go back if I wanted. My housework is a full-time job. And you never re-tire from housework."

"That's very true," I replied.

I began by outlining my plan of action. "As I am sure Dave told you, today we will go through what I call Life Goal Planning. I covered most of the preliminary stuff with Dave last weekend, so today we will jump right into it. I have been running this workshop for many years and can assure you that it is easy to apply.

"The truth is," I said, "you already have a pretty good idea how it works but in a different context. To start your thinking on this process imagine that it is the middle of a dreary winter. To brighten things up, you decide to take a holiday in the sun. So you go to a travel agent who greets you with a big smile and a warm handshake. After dispensing with the preliminaries, he asks you where you would like to go. You tell him that you are not sure, but that you thought about going to Florida. So he pulls out a book of hotel listings, shows you a few photos of several hotels, and quotes the price including return airfare. Then, after giving you a few minutes to read the descriptions, he asks, "Would you like me to book the holiday?"

"Now let's look at a different agent. This agent goes beyond asking where you would like to go. She asks you a few pertinent questions about your needs, likes and dislikes, interests, budget, and what you expect from your holiday. After determining these details, suppose she comes up with a different destination, a cruise for example that had never occurred to you. In addition, let's assume that a cruise turns out to be far superior to the original destination you had in mind.

"The difference between the two travel agents is how they went about determining your destination. The first agent failed to clarify your destination. He did not provide any service that you could not have found in a Web site or travel brochure. The second agent took the time to gather a clear understanding of your needs. She realized that your actual destination was not a specific city or location, but the satisfaction of your needs. Then she found you a destination that would enable you to satisfy your needs.

"A travel agent's job is easy when it comes to defining the client's destination. Yours may take a little work. But it will be worth it because knowing where you are heading, having a clear understanding of your re-tirement destination or objective, is a necessary starting point in your re-tirement career. Besides, if you don't know where you are heading there is no point in setting out, you can't make any plans or corrections along the way, and how will you know if you get there? As I explained to Dave last weekend, the way you perceive or look at re-tirement can influence how you approach it. So it is essential that everyone has a clear understanding of their re-tirement destination."

I asked the group to think about where they want to go or hope to gain from re-tirement, and after a few moments of silence, Dave replied, "I guess you could say that I have no idea of where I am heading."

"Join the club," said Les.

There was a long pause and then Diane said, "We like to travel."

I replied, "We are looking for an objective or destination that could apply to all re-tirees."

Most people do not have a clear understanding of their objective or destination in re-tirement. In fact, based on my workshop experience I would estimate that only about one-third of pre-re-tirees have clear-cut formulated re-tirement plans. When asked this question, the common reply is to list activities such as travel, spending more time with the grandchildren, starting a small business, spending the winters in a warm climate, and so on. However, specific activities are not your objective. Travel, golf, hobbies, volunteering, etc., are activities or vehicles that some people use as a means to reach their objective or destination in re-tirement. Another problem with focusing on activities is if for some reason you can't pursue a particular activity, you could have a problem.

We are looking for a re-tirement objective that applies to all re-tirees, regardless of age, sex, marital status, financial level, or type of occupation from which they re-tired. As I mentioned to Dave earlier, many people haven't truly thought out where they are heading in re-tirement either because they assume it will take care of itself or they don't know how to go about it.

To help them answer this question, I said, "The problem is, you are overlooking the obvious. The one re-tirement objective that everyone shares is to enjoy themselves. They want a life that is worthwhile, enjoyable, and purposeful."

"That's certainly true," said Janice.

"It's hard to disagree with this," I said. "In fact this objective can apply at all stages of life; the only difference is in re-tirement you have control over your life and your chance of reaching this objective is greater.

"Obviously, concepts such as enjoyment, worthwhile, and purpose mean different things to different people. Some things that I consider enjoyable or worthwhile may not apply to you, and vice versa. Over the years running hundreds of re-tirement workshops, I have learned that everyone is unique and I try whenever possible to be value free and not impose my likes and dislikes on others. Whether or not something is enjoyable, worthwhile, or purposeful depends entirely on the meaning these concepts have for you. Life Goal Planning is based on this assumption.

"Having established that your destination is to enjoy yourself," I continued, "the next question is, how will you get there? What do you have to do to ensure that your re-tirement will be worthwhile and enjoyable? As Dave and I discussed last week, although money is important, money alone will not guarantee re-tirement happiness. You may be well off financially, but this will not ensure that you will enjoy your re-tirement."

"I would agree with that," said Les.

To take this issue to the next level, I asked Dave for a few sheets of paper and asked everyone to write the heading 'Miss from Work' on the top of the page. I continued, "The question I would like you to think about is what will you miss from work when you re-tire. Les and Janice, because you are re-tired, think about what you miss from work. For example, you might miss contact with people or the stimulation. Don't include things that you are quite happy to give up, such as office politics or having to work late."

I gave them a few minutes to complete their list and then I pulled out a sheet that had the responses from the re-tired physicians' survey to the same question about what they miss from work.

As they wrote their lists, I jotted a few notes on a sheet of paper and after a few minutes said, "Before we look at your lists, take a look at my list (Figure 2-1)."

"How does my list compare to yours?" I asked.

"It's practically identical," replied Les.

"Why do you think I was so clever and knew your answers in advance?"

Figure 2-1

Miss From Work

Social interaction
Stimulation
Challenge
Purpose
Identity

"I guess it's because you have done this before," said Janice.

"I certainly have, every time I run my workshop and it was a key question in or re-tiree survey. Let's take a closer look at what we have. First of all, Dave and Diane, if you are concerned about giving up anything on your lists when you re-tire, or Les and Janice if you feel you are missing anything on your lists, you can console yourself knowing it is a common concern.

"To analyze your answers, thinking about what you would miss when you re-tire, you are in fact listing your reasons for enjoying work. Work is enjoyable because it is a source of friendships, achievement, challenge, and so on. However, the most important thing you can learn from your list is it identifies your needs satisfied by work. In other words, work is enjoyable because it satisfies your need for friendships, achievement, challenge, and so on.

"You have just made an important perceptual leap. Your focus has shifted from work as an activity, to your needs satisfied by work. By focusing on personal needs, we can explain, for example, why two people could do the identical job, but one enjoys it more than the other does. The activity is the same for both people but it satisfies more needs for one person compared to the other. It also explains why work may have been more enjoyable in the past compared to today. It may have satisfied more needs in the past. The work may be the same today, but its ability to satisfy your needs, say for challenge and stimulation, may have diminished. So we have to look at an activity's ability to satisfy our needs, to understand why it is or is not enjoyable."

Table 2-1 includes what your re-tirement mentors missed from practicing dentistry, followed by a few commednts. Notice that 31% missed nothing. Although many of the items may not come as a surprise, the key to re-tirement happiness is to replace these satisfactions lost from dentistry.

Table 2-1. Miss From Work

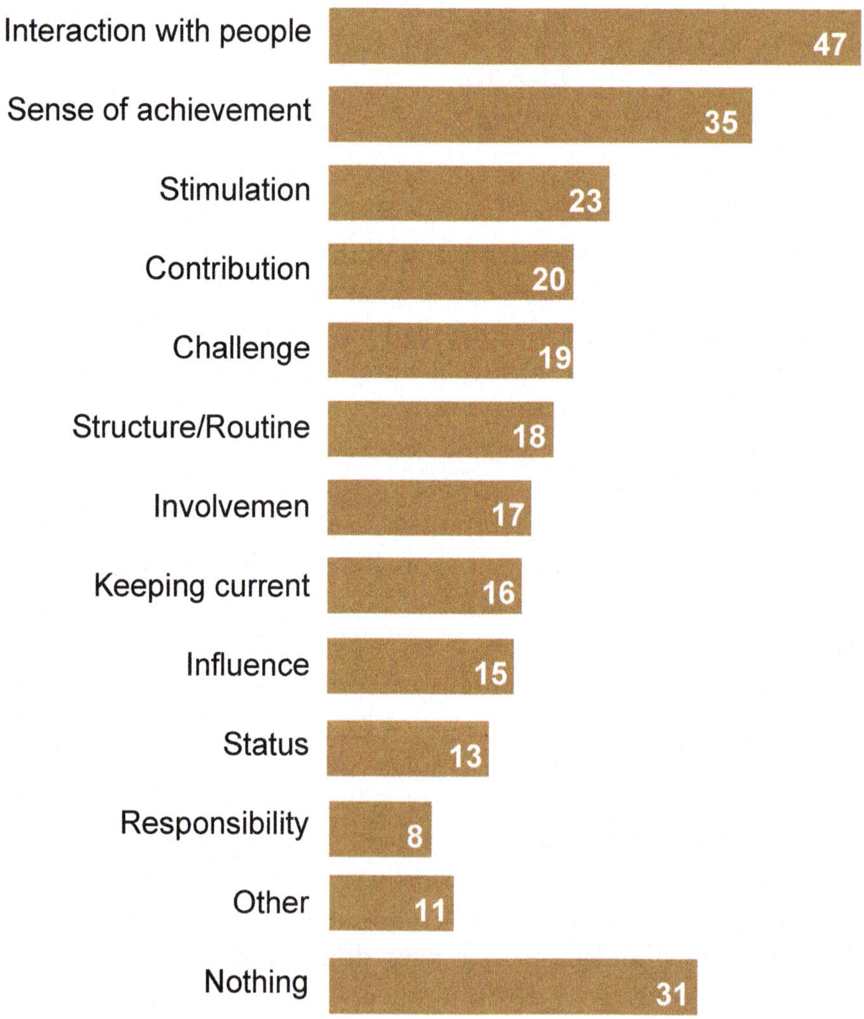

I cannot fully retire until I figure out how to replace the energy I get from work. I have saved enough money but energy is a perishable item. It can't be stored up in an account. Another concern is about becoming invisible. For 30 years I have been well respected.

Biggest "miss" are old friends, but making new friends is a challenge both my wife & I are embracing.

We were close to the point where I could reveal the secret to re-tirement happiness, but first it was necessary to expand their understanding of the relationship between satisfying needs through different activities.

"Let's take a look at this from a different angle," I said. "Suppose a young person, we'll call him Michael, enjoys playing soccer. The question is, what is it about soccer that he likes? For example, he might like the camaraderie, being with friends. Can you think of anything else he might like about soccer?

Les said, "I suppose the competition and the physical activity."

"OK," I replied. "Let's put this on paper." (See Figure 2-3)

Figure 2-3

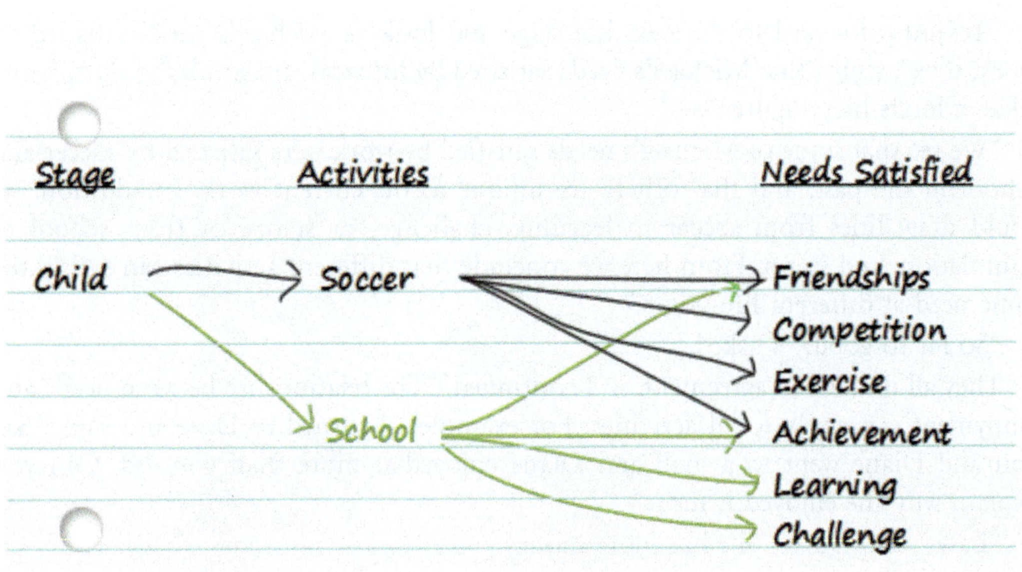

I continued. "As we discussed earlier, we can interpret Michael's reasons for enjoying soccer as his needs satisfied by soccer. In other words, he enjoys soccer because it satisfies his need for friendships, competition, exercise, and achievement. This reveals two important points. First, we enjoy activities because they satisfy our needs, and a single activity can satisfy more than one need. The more complex the activity the more needs it is likely to satisfy. Work, for example, generally satisfies many more needs than watching television. Yet even watching TV could satisfy more than one need, such as filling spare time, entertainment, keeping up on current events. In addition, if you have absolute control over the remote, it can satisfy your need for power!

"Let's introduce another activity. Besides playing sports, Michael goes to school. This is a completely different activity, but if we include his reasons for enjoying school, Michael tells us that he enjoys learning, challenge, friends, and achievement."

I added this new activity to the original sheet (fortunately I brought a few colored pens).

"The main point is that some of Michael's needs can be met by completely different activities, while others may only be met by one activity. For example, his need for friendship and achievement are satisfied through both soccer and school, while in our example his other needs are only met by one activity. Of course, we could draw a line from sports to challenge and so on. For other young people, the pattern may be different.

"To jump forward to the next life stage and look at Michael's needs satisfied by work, if we assume that Michael's needs satisfied by his work are similar to ours, here's what it looks like (Figure 2-4)."

"We see that some of Michael's needs satisfied by work were satisfied by soccer and school in the past, and that others are unique to his current work. In addition, we could draw lines from soccer to learning, challenge, or status, or from school to stimulation, and so on. From here we conclude that different activities can satisfy the same need at different life stages."

"So far so good?" I asked.

They all nodded in agreement, so I continued. "The relationship between needs and enjoyment can apply to all activities. For example," I turned to Dave and said, "Say you and Diane went to a mall and Diane enjoyed it more than you did. Can you explain why she enjoyed it more?"

"Easy," said Dave. "She has more money."

Figure 2-4

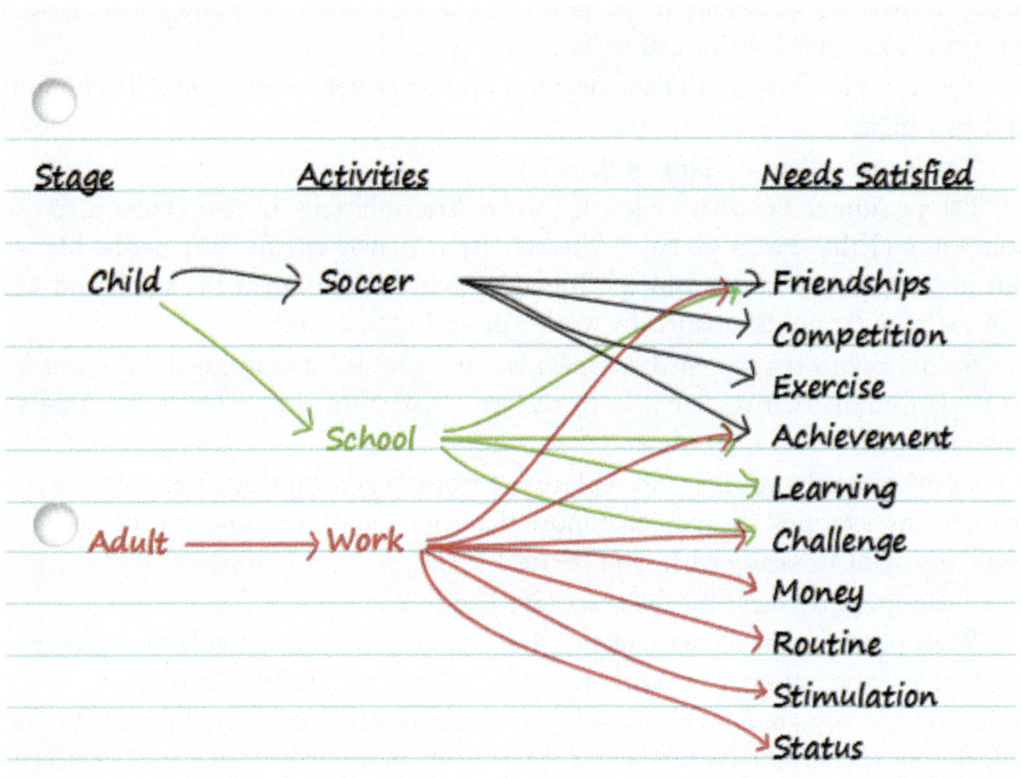

"Seriously." I said. "The reason she might enjoy shopping at the mall more than you is because it satisfies more of her needs compared to yours."

"That's for sure," said Dave.

"The same can be said for something you enjoy Dave, but Diane doesn't. It may satisfy more of your needs than Diane's."

We can interpret these examples from the perspective of Situational Analysis (discussed earlier). As explained, people respond not only to the objective features of the situation, but also to the meaning, that situation has for them. Therefore, in a situation where Dave and Diane are at the mall, it is more enjoyable to Diane than to Dave, because her definition of the situation (shopping) includes the satisfaction of more needs.

We had reached the point where I could reveal the secret to re-tirement happiness. It should have been obvious at this point so I asked if anybody could guess the secret, based on what they had learned so far.

"Yes, don't let Dave and Diane near a shopping center," said Janice. "It's bound to end in a fight."

"That's one way of looking at it," I replied.

"Let me summarize what we learned so far. Your objective in re-tirement is to enjoy yourself, and the reason we enjoy any activity is that it satisfies our needs. Many of our needs could be satisfied by a different activity at a different life stage, and when you re-tire, your needs satisfied by work will no longer be met.

"So the key to re-tirement happiness is quite simple," I continued. "All you have to do is find alternative activities to replace satisfactions lost from work. That's all there is to it."

"In other words, you have to replace the word 'work' on this sheet with the word 're-tirement activities' - it may take more than one - and draw lines to the needs and skills you want to satisfy when you re-tire.

I included re-tirement on the sheet (See Figure 2-5).

"With the freedom of re-tirement," I continued, "if you are able to satisfy more needs than those satisfied by work, life will be more enjoyable in re-tirement. On the other hand, if you are not able to satisfy your needs lost from work, life in re-tirement will not be as enjoyable as life before re-tirement. In a nutshell, that is the essence of Life Goal Planning and the key to re-tirement happiness.

"I told you it was simple, and the beauty is, it works. Remember, your objective is not specific activities, but to satisfy your needs, especially those lost from work. Re-tirement activities are simply vehicles through which you can satisfy your needs."

I waited for this to sink in and said, "What do you think? Does it make sense so far?"

Les was the first to respond. "It makes a lot of sense. I realize now that I was searching frantically for things to do but really didn't know what I was looking for. I didn't think about my needs. I took an art course, but I didn't enjoy it and I'm a lousy artist. Somebody suggested I do volunteer work, but it doesn't really appeal to me. A few of my re-tired friends seem to be having a great time. It's frustrating."

"It makes sense to me too," said Diane. "At the retirement (without the dash) seminar we attended, they talked about how important it was to find things to do in retirement. But they didn't explain it this way."

"Sounds real good in theory," said Dave. "But how does it work in reality?"

Figure 2-5

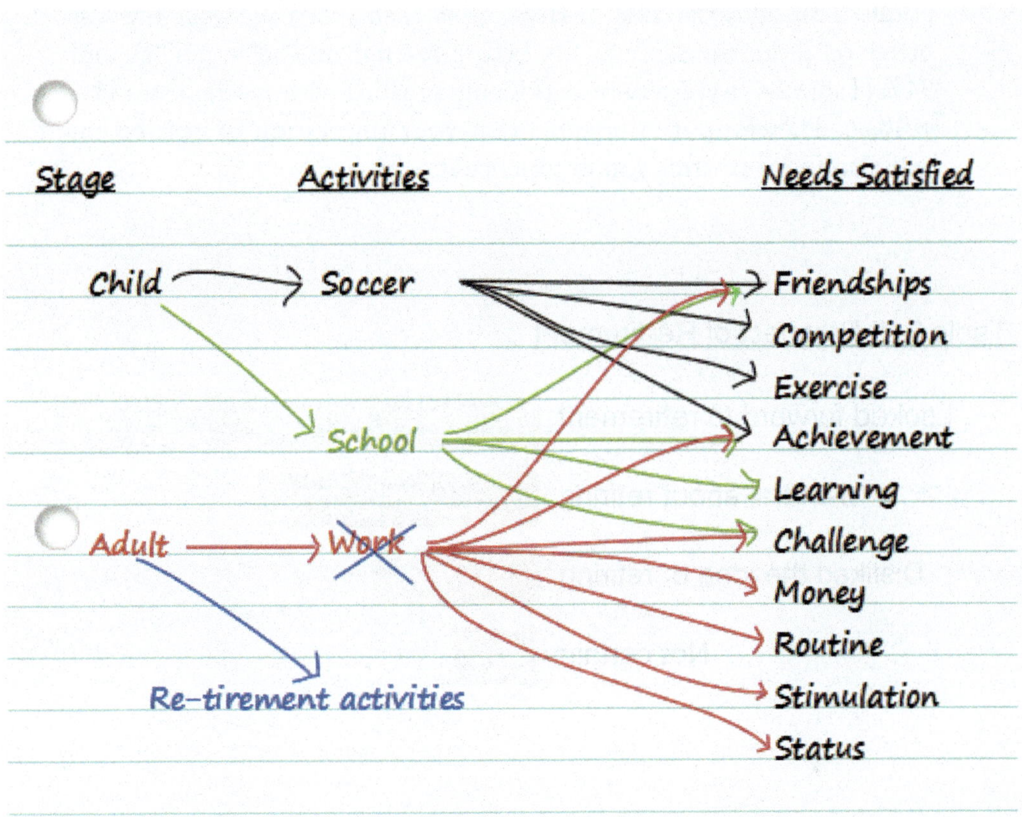

"Now that you know the secret to re-tirement happiness and the theory behind the secret, I can give you an overview of a process designed to help you create a re-tirement that you will consider enjoyable and worthwhile."

Impressions of Re-tirement

For an overview of re-tirement from the experience of our re-tired dentists, we can look at how they felt about the prospect of re-tiring just before they re-tired, how they compared life after re-tirement to life before re-tirement, how satisfied they were with re-tirement.

The data shows that the majority of our re-tirees consider re-tirement to be a positive experience and only a minority is dissatisfied. It also seems that opinions of re-tirement can actually improve after re-tirement. Before they re-tired 51% looked forward to re-tirement (Table 2-2), but after they re-tired, 92% (Table 2-3) felt that life was better or about the same as life before re-tirement (56% + 36%), and 94% (Table 2-4) were very or reasonably satisfied with re-tirement (54% + 40%). Therefore, it is possible that your impression of re-tirement will also improve after you experience it.

Table 2-2. Prospect of Re-tirement

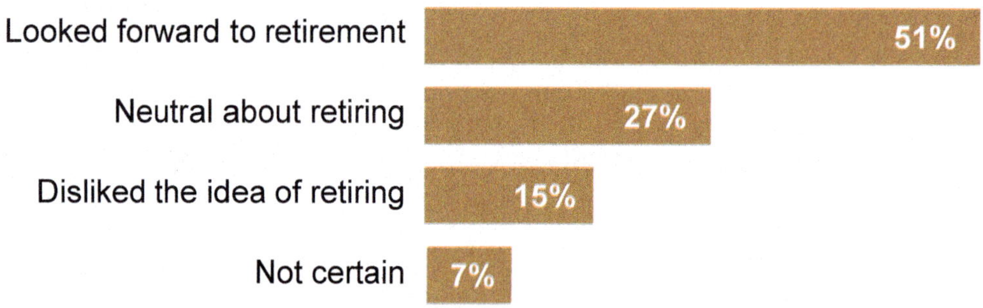

Table 2-3. Life Before and After Re-tirement

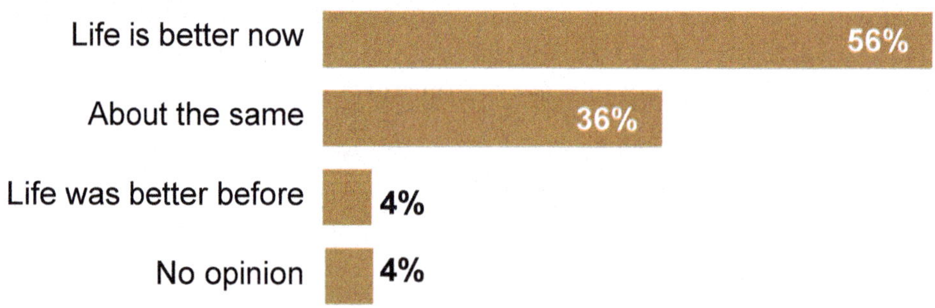

Table 2-4. Satisfaction with Re-tirement

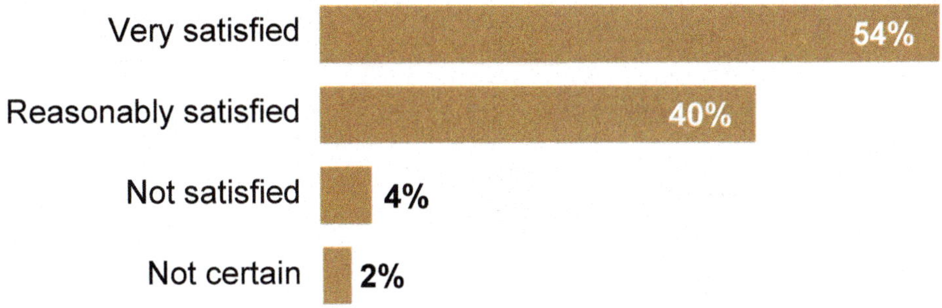

To gain a different perspective the survey included several open-ended or qualitative questions giving your re-tirement mentors free reign to elaborate on the main attractions and drawbacks of re-tirement. This perspective revealed several important underling issues and concerns that the quantitative responses had not necessarily identified. The responses to each question ranged widely, but they present an excellent perspective from people with first hand re-tirement experience.

The Main Attractions of Re-tirement

When asked to describe the main attractions of re-tirement, they were presented with an open-ended questions so they could respond without restrictions. As presented in Table 2-5, three general categories emerged. The main advantage or attraction of re-tirement, not surprisingly, is the freedom it brings and the opportunity to pursue your own interests. Push factors include things about dentistry that they were quite happy to give up - things that in a sense pushed them into re-tirement like deadlines, stress, or responsibilities. Pull factors, include specific activities they enjoyed in re-tirement - things that pulled them into re-tirement.

Table 2-5. Attractions of Re-tirement

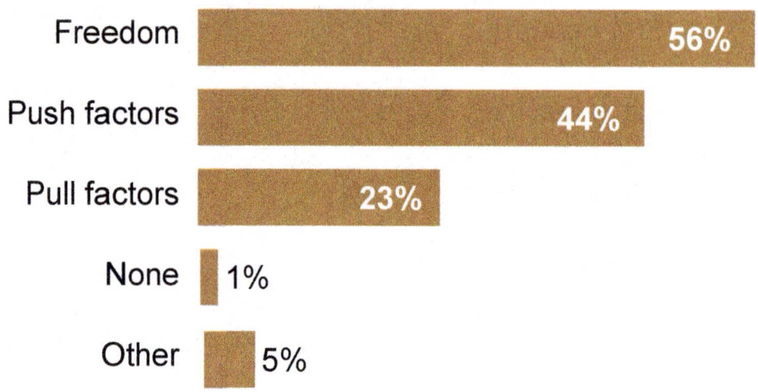

To look beyond the number, here are a few direct quotes in each category.

Freedom

References to freedom implied the opportunity to do as you choose, which often stands in direct contrast to work. For example:

To plan my day filled with what I want to do rather than plan around work schedules, planned time off, and needs of my patients. Spending time with family and activities I let go to focus on actively practicing dentistry.

Freedom to do what I want when I want. Less stress. Less drama. fewer interactions with bureaucrats and insurance.

You now control your life and have given up all the responsibility.

Total independence from time constraints. Leisure time to spend with family and pursuing hobbies.

Time to do things that were put off due to lack of time.

Do what I want when I want. Not chasing the clock all day.

Push Factors

Another attraction of retirement is the relief it can bring from the stress and pressures of practicing dentistry. According to your retirement mentors, life in retirement can be more peaceful and relaxing, less stressful, and you can please yourself without feeling guilty. This category includes references to things about practicing dentistry that your retirement mentors were happy to leave behind. Things like, patient demands, responsibilities, shift work, government red tape, administrative tasks, and so on. For example:

Freedom from schedule obligations. Less stress from practice administration (dental insurance and staff).

Freedom from the negatives of patient care...complaints, obligations, interruptions.

Less stress, less conflict, time to be unstructured, less sense of responsibility, not hurting people, able to try new things and experiences.

Having free time to explore for the future is a plus. It's exciting to reinvent your life. While running a business was very interesting and challenging, I don't miss all the minutia created by formal regulations (labor laws, OSHA). In retirement there is less stress for me.

Having time to myself and not being a slave to a schedule and to people I might not like. Worry about overhead and staff interactions.

Reduced stress. Freedom from a schedule Not dealing with employees and their problems. Freedom to pursue any interests I wish.

Knowing that I no longer have to make all of the work related decisions on a daily basis. I also do not have to concern myself that health benefits are provided and worry about the ebb and flow of cash to cover all of the expenses related to private practice.

Pull Factors

The pull factors include specific interests or activities the individual looked forward to pursuing in re-tirement. Some examples are; the opportunity to travel, spend more time with family, hobbies, sports, take on new or additional challenges, volunteer work, move to a new location, socialize, service clubs, and so on.

More time with family, friends and colleagues Administrative responsibilities are minimal To continue to be of service to patients. Continue my education to provide current best practices for their care.

As long as you are healthy, it's an opportunity to pursue anything you want but it's a great opportunity to go back to school for any goal: pursue a hobby, learn something you have always wanted to do but had no time, 'second career....

Relaxation, travel without restrictions, hobby pursuit, visiting children, time with spouse, general freedom.

More time with friends and family. More time to travel Working on my sense of humor.

Pursuing hobbies without time pressures. in general taking things a bit slower. more time to be a grandparent.

Reading the paper, not just the headlines. Fewer mulligans, better golf. More soccer games and grand kids activities. More traveling.

Drawbacks of Re-tirement

To balance the equation, the survey included a question about the drawbacks of re-tirement. Replies to this question fell into six categories as on Table 2-6. We see that 41% mentioned social and psychological losses and that 20% said there were no drawbacks to retirement.

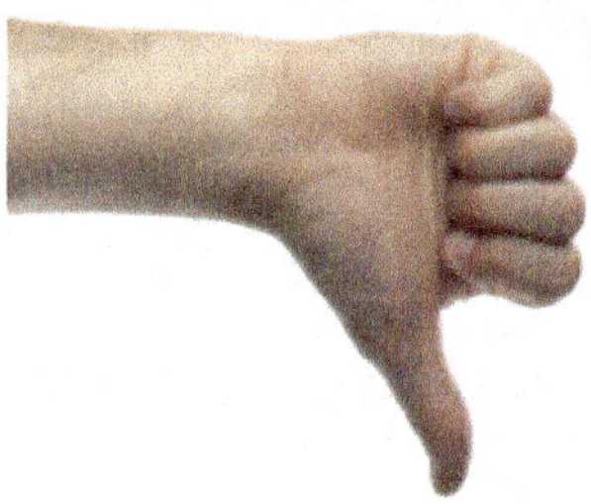

Table 2-6. Drawbacks of Retirement

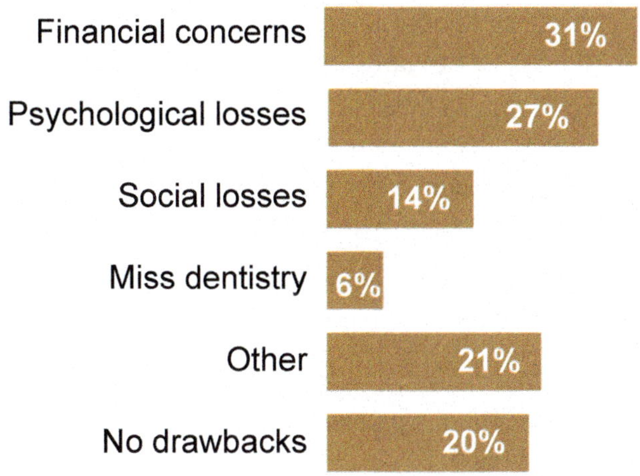

Financial Concerns

No matter when you re-tire - good times or bad - your income is likely to be reduced and you may have to learn how to budget your money. As several people mentioned, good financial planning helps.

The need to be more far looking in planning income stream and understanding that there are world economic variables that are totally out of my control.

Lack of chance of recovery financially in the event of national or world-wide financial changes that could impact my financial situation and perhaps require a reduction in lifestyle.

Not enough money, nothing left to enjoy normal life!!! Social security benefits in this country worse than third world countries.

The cash flow slows tremendously, but the bills keep right on rolling in. I plan to live as I currently do for a while. My house is too big for me and I need time to downsize and sell. (My state) is NOT a great place to retire, because the state runs mostly on property taxes, which don't take one's work status into consideration at all. If I lived in a state that has an income tax, I'd save at least a few thousand yearly.

Psychological Losses

Psychological losses include feeling of boredom, lack of intellectual stimulation, lack of daily structure or routine, reduced motivation, lack of identity, purpose, and so on. 27% of respondents mentioned this, and it is something to look out for.

We all identify ourselves as dentists, helping people. Unless we can find another outlet for our drive and creative ambitions we are going to feel lost and unfulfilled.

A diminished feeling of accomplishment & being a worthwhile contributor to society.

lack of structure lack of project completion No longer having access to the energy people bring to the office.

Less structure. I LIKE to work and be busy doing something constructive-that is why I go overboard with volunteer work now that I am in the office only 2 days a week. I need something to get up for in the morning.

The loss of patients' appreciation for the care you've given (less ego-feeding)

Unless you pursue a passion from before or one newly discovered you will rust and decay and fall into disrepair. Essentially challenges will appear to your physical, mental, spiritual, and emotional well being and whatever time you have left on this earth becomes a challenge sometimes overwhelming robbing you of the fullness this life has to offer. Nobody said this life was easy but for sure as you retire it can provide opportunities for your growth and happiness that you never envisioned as a loving and caring person and provide relationships anew and enrich others.

Social Losses

Giving up contact with patients and colleagues is another important drawback mentioned by our research subjects.

Loss of socialization and interactions with others. Being looked up to by others...having less status.

Missing the personal contact with the patients that you have had through a 36 year career. The feeling in retirement of not being a productive member of society.

Because I am a young retiree, a lot of my friends are still working full time and this limits interaction with them.

conversing with the varied patients was stimulating, made time for knowing my patients and vice versa

Miss Dentistry

I miss treating the patient population. Serving the needs of patients needing care. Training younger doctors and sharing my over the years expertise.

I loved dentistry and wish it were more a part of my life.

Leaving a profession I have loved.

Slight sense that patients felt abandoned - not a huge thing though.

Out of the dental loop. Not being able to participate in new dental advances.

Chapter Summary

- Your main objective in re-tirement is that life will be enjoyable, worthwhile and purposeful.
- The reason we enjoy any activity is because it satisfies our needs. Often the same need can be met by a different activity, at the same or or a different life stage.
- The key to re-tirement happiness is to find alternative activities that will continue to satisfy your needs and skills that were satisfied by your work.
- The main things your re-tirement mentors missed from dentistry included peer and patient interaction, a sense of achievement, contribution, involvement, keeping current and stimulation.
- The majority looked forward to re-tirement, felt that life in re-tirement was better or about the same as life before re-tirement, and were very or reasonably satisfied with retirement.
- The main attractions of re-tirement included freedom, the opportunity to pursue personal interests, and the absence of deadlines, stress or work responsibilities.
- The main drawbacks included financial concerns, social losses, and psychological losses such as feeling of boredom, lack of intellectual stimulation, lack of daily structure or routine, reduced motivation, lack of identity, and purpose.

TICKETS
TICKETS
NO REFUNDS
NO REFUNDS
NO REFUNDS

3

TICKET TO RIDE

(The Beatles, 1965)

LIFE GOAL PLANNING OVERVIEW

This chapter includes a brief overview of the Life Goal Planning process. Complete instructions and worksheets are available in Part 3, at the end of the book. I recommend you read this chapter to get an idea of how the process works, and then complete the workshop yourself or with a small group of friends/relatives.

Due to time constraints, I was not able to go through the complete workshop. To give them a general understanding of the process, I began by saying, "To set the record straight, because everyone's needs and interests are different, Life Goal Planning will not tell you what you should do in re-tirement. What may appeal to me may not appeal to you, and vice versa. However, it will, give you something much more valuable - the tools to make your re-tirement worthwhile and enjoyable.

"First of all, you have to realize that the perfect re-tirement activities will not fall into your lap; it might take time to find them. When I refer to perfect, I mean activities that will replace your needs and skills lost from work. In addition, by referring to activities in the plural, I am acknowledging that it may take several activities to accomplish this. Second, you may have to experiment with several different activities before you find the ones that are perfect for you."

To help them understand the process I gave them an example that I often use in my workshop.

"When you go sailing," I said. "You know your destination. It could be across the lake, the ocean, or to return to where you started. What you don't know is the route you will take. If the winds are favorable, if they are steady, you set the sails once and head straight for your destination. If the winds are shifting, which is usually the case, you have to tack, or follow a zigzag course to reach your destination.

"The same process applies to Life Goal Planning. Remember, your destination is not a specific activity like travel, playing golf, or getting a job. Activities are vehicles through which you can satisfy your needs. Your destination or objective is to replace satisfactions (needs and skills) lost from work. If the conditions are favorable and your re-tirement plans or activities enable you to satisfy your needs and skills, then you have reached your destination. You do not have to make any adjustments. If conditions are not favorable, if your plans do not satisfy all your needs and skills, you are going to have to experiment with different activities to reach your destination."

"Life Goal Planning involves several stages. So far, we have dealt mainly with concepts and theory. Now we will apply the secret to re-tirement happiness in the real world. Today you will learn how to identify your needs and skills and how to evaluate activities based on those needs and skills. Dave and Diane, you can apply this to your future re-tirement plans. Les and Janice, you can apply this to your re-tirement. Then I will show you how to come up with new plans. This can be valuable before or after you re-tire."

I have met many people in my corporate and public workshops who know exactly what they want to do when they re-tire. Well, that may be so. However, conditions may change, or what they thought would be worthwhile may turn out to be the opposite. Time and time again, I come across people who became disenchanted with re-tirement after the initial 'honeymoon' phase ended. They got the travel bug out of their system, or they found that playing golf everyday was not as much fun as they thought it would be. So, whether you have plans for re-tirement or not, it is important that you take the time to evaluate what you will do with yourself in the future - just in case.

Also people whose main occupation is housework, I acknowledge that one rarely re-tires from this line of work. Life Goal Planning is just as relevant. The only difference is to think in the context of housework rather than paid work. Occasionally I have met a spouse with the attitude, and I paraphrase, "I am just here because of my husband." Re-tirement is a shared experience that can affect both partners. The more knowledgeable both partners are about re-tirement, the more likely the transition will be successful.

"OK. Let's get started," said Les, anxiously.

To start the process I said, "The first thing you have to realize is this process may take some time. You may come up with an inspiration today that serves you well throughout your re-tirement career. On the other hand, it is more likely that you will have to experiment with different activities until you reach your destination. Remember, you are attempting to replace satisfactions lost from work, and this can be a tall order. Having said that, if you keep applying the Life Goal Planning process, you may be able to reach your destination sooner, rather than later."

Develop Your Needs and Skills List

"Given that your objective or destination in re-tirement is to satisfy your needs and skills, especially those lost from work, your first task is obvious. You have to find out what these are. You have to clarify your destination by developing a Needs and Skills List to determine exactly what it is that you have to replace. You can accomplish this quite simply by answering a few questions about your work and leisure. The complete program includes seven questions and the more information you gather about your needs and skills, the more you have to work with. Today we will look at three questions. This should give you a good start and you can continue the process later on your own.

"The first question focuses on needs at work. We looked at this earlier when I asked you to write down what you missed from work. If you recall, the things you might miss turned out to be your needs satisfied by work. So take a piece of paper and on the left side write the heading 'Needs & Skills'. Dave and Diane transfer your list of things you will miss when you re-tire, and Les and Janice transfer the things you miss in re-tirement, to your new list. At the same time, you might add a few new things that you hadn't thought of originally. Take a few minutes to do this exercise because these are the main things you may have to replace when you re-tire."

After allowing a few minutes to complete this question, I said, "When I spoke about replacing satisfactions lost from work, I was referring to both needs and skills. Your list must also include your skills because part of the reason we enjoy an activity is because it gives us the opportunity to use our skills. In addition, skills are transferable. You may use some of your work skills in a completely different re-tirement activity. So think about your skills at work and add them to your list under your needs satisfied by work.

"To help you think about your skills, sometimes we take our skills for granted because they may be second nature. So imagine that you had to find your replacement when you re-tire and ask yourself what skills you would look for in your replacement."

After they added work skills to their lists I said, "There is more to life than work and if you are interested in uncovering your needs, you should also look at leisure. After all, you freely choose leisure activities and we generally choose those we enjoy. Therefore, they can provide excellent clues to your needs. So on the next line of your list after your work skills, write down an activity that you do for leisure, and then below that, list your reasons for enjoying that activity. Thinking about your reasons for enjoying leisure is very important because it identifies your needs satisfied by that activity. Do this for several leisure activities if you can. When you finish I will show you how you can put your Needs and Skills List to work."

After a little discussion, they were ready for the second stage of the process.

"Although we haven't answered all the questions from my workshop (see all seven questions in the Appendix) you have created something valuable," I explained. "To prove this, let me ask you a question. How many of you would agree that if all the items on your list were met when you re-tired, your re-tirement would be worthwhile and enjoyable?"

In unison, they agreed.

"In that case," I said, "you possess something of value that most people do not have when they re-tire. You know your destination or objective in re-tirement. Your destination is to satisfy the items on your Needs and Skills List. Think of your list as a wish list for re-tirement. If you satisfy the items on your list your re-tirement will be worthwhile and enjoyable."

Evaluate Re-tirement Plans

The next stage involves using the list of needs and skills to evaluate re-tirement plans. Although the process is the same, it differs slightly if one is re-tired or not. I turned to Dave and Diane and said, "You now have a brief list of your needs and skills, and you agreed that if these items were met when you re-tire, then your re-tirement will be worthwhile and enjoyable. So now, you can use this as a benchmark to evaluate your plans. Les and Janice, you can use the same evaluation process to determine what is missing from your re-tirement.

"Here's how it works," I continued. "Dave and Diane take a look at your list of needs and skills and ask yourselves if each item will be met to your satisfaction given your re-tirement plans. Go through each item and place a 'Y' next to those needs or skills that you expect will be met, an 'N' next to those that will not be met, and a question mark next to those that you are not sure of because you may have to wait until you re-tire.

"Les and Janice do the same, but because you are re-tired your evaluation will be based not on what you expect, but on your current experiences. Therefore, in your case there will be no question marks. You don't have to wait to see if a need or skill will be met, you are re-tired."

I asked Dave and Diane if they identified a need or skill that would not be met when they re-tire.

"I found a few," said Diane.

"The problem is," said Dave. "I really don't have any plans, so I don't have much to work with."

"That's OK," I replied. "Because soon I will show you how to come up with new plans."

I turned to Les and Janice and asked the same question.

"I can see quite a few things that are missing," said Les. "It sort of gives you a whole new perspective."

"You can use this," I explained, "before or after you re-tire. This information or these insights may spark an idea that could point you in the direction of how to make your plans or current activities better."

I have many examples from my workshop of people who improved their plans as a result of this process. One was a welder who planned to re-tire to a small farm and set up a welding shop. When he evaluated his plan to move to the farm, he identified 'teaching' as an item on his Needs and Skills List that was not part of his re-tirement plans. He identified teaching as a need during the brainstorming session to follow and given his welding skill, this revelation prompted him to look into how he could satisfy this need and thereby improve his re-tirement. Although this may seem obvious in retrospect, he did not think about this prospect until he evaluated his plans based on his Needs and Skills List.

Another was a couple who planned to move to the coast and buy a condominium in a high-rise building. When they went through their list of needs and skills, the husband who loved gourmet cooking, identified items that related to this interest, and the wife identified items that related to her love of antiquing - neither of which would be enhanced with their current plan. As they pondered their situation, and with a little help from other workshop participants, they came up with the idea of purchasing a small farm in the country. This would enable him to open a gourmet restaurant and she could sell antiques. This idea opened a new world of opportunities including trips to Europe to purchase antiques.

How to Create New Plans: Brainstorming

The next stage involves a completely different process that is the starting point for creating new plans. To explain I said, "Now that you know how to evaluate your plans, it is time to learn how to come up with or create new plans. The perfect re-tirement activities, those that will satisfy your needs, will probably not just fall into your lap. You may have to create them and you have to start somewhere. Les, you mentioned that you would like to find some new interests in re-tirement, and Dave you are still pondering the question of what to do when you re-tire. So let's look at these issues. In both cases, you can use your Needs and Skills List as a starting point. This process works best with a small group, but you can do it on your own. It's based on brainstorming and here is how it works with a group.

"The objective of the brainstorming session is to receive as many re-tirement suggestions as possible. Each person takes a turn to read aloud his or her entire Needs and Skills List. Meanwhile the others are taking notes and jotting down what they think are the reader's key needs and skills. Then look at your notes and each person is responsible for coming up with a re-tirement career suggestion for that person. When a suggestion is made, and this is very important, whoever receives the suggestion should write it as given on one sheet of paper, and whoever made the suggestion should write it on his or her own sheet of paper. So everybody take a piece of paper and write, 'Suggestions Given' at the top of one sheet, and 'Suggestions Received' at the top of the other sheet."

To start the brainstorming process I asked Les, our resident re-tiree, to read his list of needs and skills aloud and for the others to take notes as he read.

When Les finished reading his list, I said, "Based on Les's needs and skills, can anyone make any suggestion of what he might do to add something new to his life?"

Dave asked, "Les, you used to restore old furniture. Do you still do it?"

"Sometimes," Les replied.

"Then why don't you put an ad in the paper to restore furniture?" Dave suggested.

I interjected at this point and said, "OK, Les you have a suggestion, so write it on your sheet headed Suggestions Received. Dave, because you made the suggestion, write it on your sheet headed Suggestions Given."

"If you say so," said Dave, but what's the use in me writing down his suggestion?"

"I will explain it to you soon," I replied. "Now, does anybody else have a suggestion for Les?"

Janice said, "Les, you could sell some of the stuff we have in the basement and garage."

Again I reminded Les to write the suggestion on his sheet, and Janice to write the suggestion she on her sheet headed 'Suggestions Given'.

Then Diane added, "Les, you mentioned public speaking as a skill. Why not see if you could teach a course on public speaking? Or, maybe you could volunteer."

"These are all excellent suggestions," I said, and reminded everyone to write the suggestion on the appropriate page.

During the brainstorming exercise, I asked them to put personal judgments and evaluations aside to allow ideas to flow. Now that each person had several ideas to work with, I let them in on an important secret that could be quite insightful for revealing additional needs and skills for their list, and in turn might help them find the perfect re-tirement. First, I asked them to take a close look at the suggestions they made to others, and asked them what they saw. They spent a few minutes pondering this question and then Les said, "Actually I see a few things here that appeal to me."

"Me too," said Diane.

"The reason for this," I explained, "is when you are making a suggestion to someone else in essence you are saying, if I were you this is what I would do. So giving suggestions to others turns out to be an excellent way to uncover additional interests and needs that apply to you."

"But the point is," I continued, "you are not the other person, but if you were, this is how you would approach it. Look closely at the suggestions you made for others. This might give you additional clues for your re-tirement. Do you see any patterns?

Did you make several suggestions that involved say starting a business, or teaching, or helping others, or joining something? If you see a pattern among the suggestions you made, or any words that appeal to you, you have identified additional needs or skills that you can add to your list.

"Now take a look at the suggestions you received. If you identify a suggestion or even part of a suggestion that appeals to you, add them to your Needs and Skills List if they are not already on your list."

Next, we looked at how to tie this all together and to demonstrate this process I asked Dave for a pitcher of water and five empty glasses.

Guide Your Re-tirement Career

To explain this process I filled four glasses with varying amounts of water and arranged them on the table in a zigzag fashion. Then I filled the fifth glass, took a drink, and set it aside. I was thirsty.

Figure 3-1

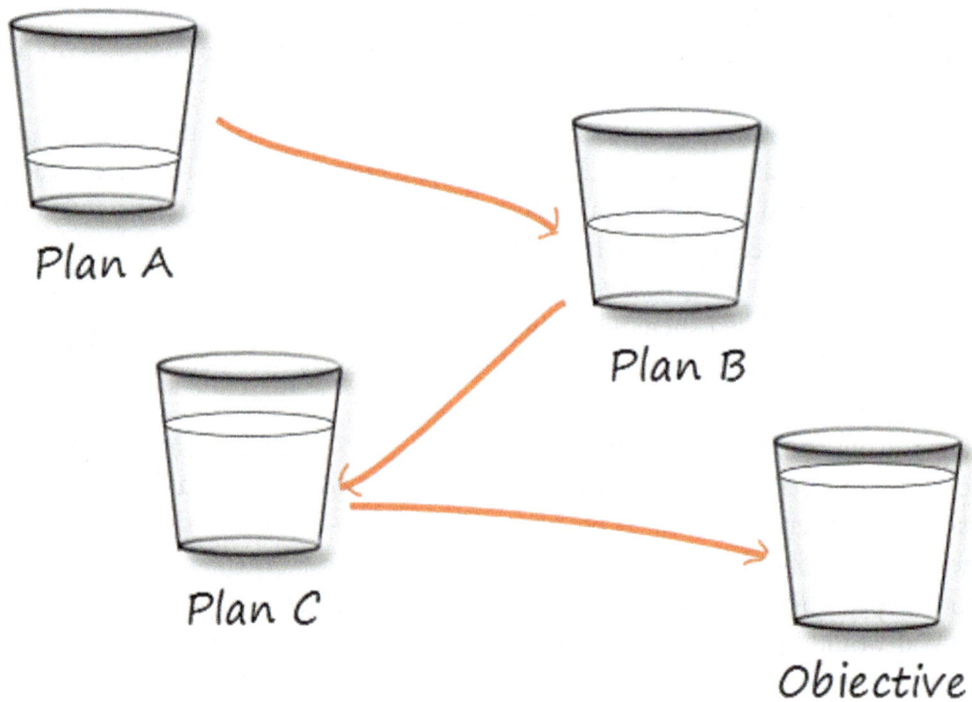

As they looked on, I explained, "To demonstrate how your re-tirement career will develop based on your needs and skills imagine that these four glasses represent your re-tirement career. The full glass represents your re-tirement objective - that is the point when you find activities that will enable you to satisfy your main needs and skills, especially those lost from work.

"After you re-tire, suppose you pursue Plan A, or if you don't have plans you start to pursue the idea from the brainstorming session that appeals to you the most. However, let's suppose you start to pursue Plan A and something is missing. You are not satisfying all your needs.

"Based on your experience in Plan A, you go back to your Needs and Skills List to determine what is missing. Then you brainstorm, as we did earlier, and come up with a new idea. This leads you to Plan B. It satisfies more needs, but still something is missing. You repeat this process until you end at the full glass where all your needs are satisfied.

"The key to this process," I emphasized, "is to understand that what you end up doing may be the furthest thing from your mind when you originally set out. However, because you did Plan A, which led to Plan B, which led to C, and ultimately you will reach your re-tirement destination where all your main needs and skills are satisfied.

"When I refer to re-tirement as a career that is exactly what I mean. It will develop and progress through several activities all building from the last until you find the perfect re-tirement activities that satisfy your needs."

To reinforce this point, I presented a hypothetical scenario incorporating the various Life Goal Planning concepts.

"Suppose my re-tirement plans - my Plan A - included spending the winters in a warm climate, finding a part-time job to top up my income, and to take up tennis with my wife. I expect that these plans will satisfy my needs. Then suppose when I pursue my plan, it doesn't quite work out. I look for a part time job but can't find anything that interests me. Although we enjoy being away in the winter, I am a bit bored, and while playing tennis I sprain my ankle.

"There is something missing from my life, and I am at the glass that is only partially full."

"Sounds a bit like me," said Les.

Janice smiled and asked if she could have a glass of water. Dave and Diane laughed at this request.

To continue with my hypothetical scenario, I said, "To improve my situation I go back to my Needs and Skills List to see what is missing. Suppose I went through my list and identified friendships as something that was missing. My ankle has healed so we decide to join a tennis club to meet new people and take tennis lessons. While at the tennis club we meet a couple, and they invite us to go hiking. This idea didn't occur to us before, but we decide to join them. It turns out we have a great time with their group on the hike so we quit the tennis club and spend most weekends hiking either with the group or just the two of us. I have reached the next glass through my revised plans. I am satisfying more needs including the need for friendships.

"I become heavily involved in the world of hiking. I develop a Web site on hiking that I can access when I am away in the winter. It includes an active chat room and I start to organize hiking trips to exotic locations. Now we are traveling to scout out potential hiking trips. Lo and behold my cup, or should I say my glass, runneth over. I have reached my destination and am satisfying all of my needs. In fact I am satisfying more needs than before I re-tired.

"The main point of my example," I continued, "is the activities that I ended up doing in re-tirement were the furthest things from my mind when I re-tired. If somebody had suggested that I become heavily involved in hiking, I would have said they were crazy. Nevertheless, because I sprained my ankle, that led to joining the tennis club, which led to meeting a couple of hikers, and so on, and so on.

"So start by picking an activity. It doesn't have to be perfect, but you have to start somewhere. Evaluate it with your Needs and Skills List. If it seems like a good idea, if it seems like it will satisfy most of your important needs, go for it. You will never know unless you try. If it doesn't work out, or if conditions change, brainstorm some new idea based on your current pursuits, evaluate it, and move on to something better. Continue this process until you reach your final destination that satisfies all of your needs and skills."

As I explained, "Your Needs and Skills List can be extremely valuable both before and after you re-tire. It can be used to evaluate plans or ideas, to come up with new ideas, and to make adjustments as you progress through your re-tirement career."

"I follow what you are saying," said Janice. "I have a friend Barbara - you know her, Diane. Anyway, she and her husband wanted to travel and spend some time living in a foreign country when they re-tired. Unfortunately, her husband took ill and they couldn't travel. What should somebody do then?"

"That's a very good question," I replied. "Like the song says, you can't always get what you want. Right now, what I want is to take a little break. If you don't mind, let's come back to this in a few minutes."

You Can't Always Get What You Want

(Rolling Stones, 1969)

After a short break, I recalled Diane's question and said, "I agree with you, Diane. It's all very well to talk about finding enjoyable and worthwhile pursuits in retirement, but what if for some reason you couldn't do what you wanted to do? Suppose you wanted to find a job but couldn't? Suppose your dreams included sailing but because of medical reasons, your spouse has to be on dry land? What if you wanted to travel but couldn't afford it?"

I answered my own question. "You can get what you want, if you find an alternative way to get there. Remember, finding a job, sailing your boat or travel are not your objectives. Your objective is to satisfy your needs. A job, sailing, and travel are activities or vehicles through which you can satisfy your needs. You can meet the same need or skill through different activities. So if you can't go sailing or find a job, determine which needs you would like to satisfy and find or create an alternative activity that will allow you to satisfy most if not all of those needs."

I told them about a couple from a workshop who wanted to move to the coast and spend time sailing their boat when they re-tired. That situation was similar to her friend Barbara's situation. Unfortunately, just before they were about to move, the wife took ill and her doctor advised against this plan. They were devastated. What could they do? They had been planning this move for a long time.

They had two options. They could abandon their plans and do nothing, or, they could look for an alternative. Realizing that their plans were to satisfy certain needs and skills, they sat down and identified those needs and skills. Then, given the wife's medical needs, they brainstormed an alternative and decided to buy a trailer and travel the coast. Although their alternative was not quite as ideal as sailing, it was nevertheless another way they could satisfy most of their travel needs, including the additional need of immediate access to health care, if necessary.

This is an important point, so I followed up with another example.

"Remember I mentioned a welder who improved his re-tirement plans when he identified teaching as one of his needs? Suppose after he moved to the farm he approached the local school to teach welding. Suppose the school didn't need a welding teacher. What do you suggest he should do?" I asked.

"He could look for another job," said Les.

"That's true," I replied. "But suppose his needs were focused more on teaching than on earning money. He wasn't after a job. He simply wanted to pass his skill on to someone else."

"Maybe he could teach somebody on his own," suggested Diane. "You said that he was going to open his own workshop. That would be perfect."

"Good suggestion Diane," I said. "His main concern was to satisfy his need to teach. If he can't do it through the school, he may be able to find an interested kid who would love to learn how to weld, and he could teach him or her on his own. On the other hand, maybe teach something else altogether. If his need to teach welding in a school was great enough, he may decide to go back to school and become a teacher. Who knows? Remember, re-tirement is a career that will develop and evolve and sometimes you never know where you will end up."

Ace up Your Sleeve

"The point is," I emphasized, "You have an ace up your sleeve. If there is something you want to do but for some reason you can't do it, you have the tools to find or create an alternative. You do not necessarily have to rely on others as you progress through your re-tirement career. This is in stark contrast to the work career experienced by most people.

"Say somebody wanted to find a job, or had a job and hated it. The same needs may be satisfied through self-employment or a nonpaying activity. If you can't afford to travel, you can organize a group and maybe have your way paid by a travel agency. On the other hand, you might travel on a freighter, or find something completely different - as long as it satisfies your needs. If for some reason you are unable to pursue anything, the process I described earlier will allow you to create a worthwhile and enjoyable alternative. Who knows, your alternative may be a blessing in disguise. It may turn out to be better than the original.

"Looking for a job is similar to looking for any activity in re-tirement, the only difference is a job satisfies (in varying degrees) an extra need, money. Remember," I added, "your destination or objective is to satisfy your needs. If for some reason you can't participate in one activity, simply find an alternative activity to satisfy those needs. This simple fact is at the heart of a successful re-tirement career. You have the time, and now you have the tools to create a future that will be worthwhile and enjoyable. All you have to do is put them to work."

Chapter Summary

- Given that the key to re-tirement happiness is to replace your needs and skills satisfied by work, the first step in Life Goal Planning is to identify your needs and skills, i.e. create your Life Goal List.
- Your Life Goal List identifies the conditions that will make your re-tirement worthwhile and enjoyable.
- This creates a benchmark against which you can test your re-tirement plans to identify a Life Goal shortfall and perhaps improve your plans.
- Your Life Goal List can also be used to compare different plans to see which plan is likely to satisfy more of your needs and skills.
- Should it be necessary to create new plans, your Life Goal List can be used as a basis or starting point to brainstorm new ideas.
- Finally you can use your Life Goal List to guide your re-tirement career so that eventually your re-tirement will be worthwhile and enjoyable.
- If there is something you want to do but for some reason you can't do it, you have the tools to find or create an alternative activity that will satisfy your needs.

PART 2

Other Lifestyle Issues

4

A HARD DAY'S NIGHT

(The Beatles, 1964)

WORKING IN RE-TIREMENT

Working in re-tirement is not for everyone, however it is not uncommon for people to think about this prospect. Even if you do not plan to work in re-tirement, this issue can provide insights into your re-tirement career. Before we deal with this issue, let's look at your re-tirement mentors.

Fifty-three percent of your re-tirement mentors worked for a salary or other compensation since re-tiring. Of these, 89% worked part-time and 90% worked in dentistry related activities. To look a little deeper, there are various reasons why people seek work in re-tirement. On the one hand, some may have felt a financial pinch in re-tirement and felt the need to earn extra money. On the other hand, some may have felt bored and looked for work to relieve this situation. To test these differences, those people who worked in re-tirement were asked if their reasons for working were mainly financial or non-financial (Table 4-1), and to identify the main non-financial reasons for working in retirement (Table 4-2).

From Table 4-1, we see that only 12% worked in re-tirement strictly for the money. Table 4-2 confirms the non-monetary benefits as reasons for working in re-tirement. This is also consistent with the things they missed from work as outlined in Chapter 2, namely, peer and patient interaction, achievement, challenge, and so on. We can conclude, therefore, that working in re-tirement usually serves as a vehicle to replace non-monetary satisfactions lost from work.

Table 4-1. Financial vs. Non-financial Reasons For Working

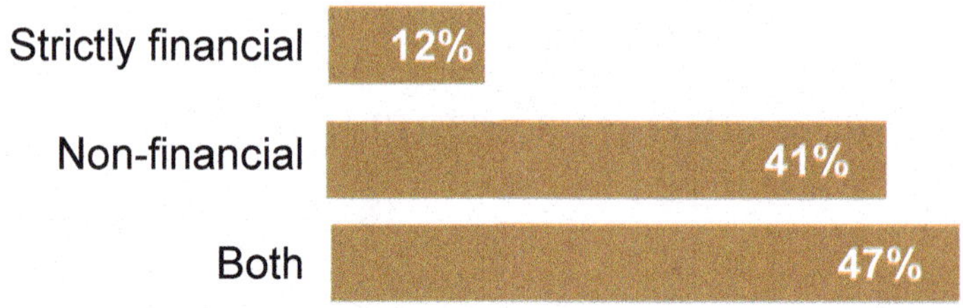

Table 4-2. Main Reasons For Working in Re-tirement

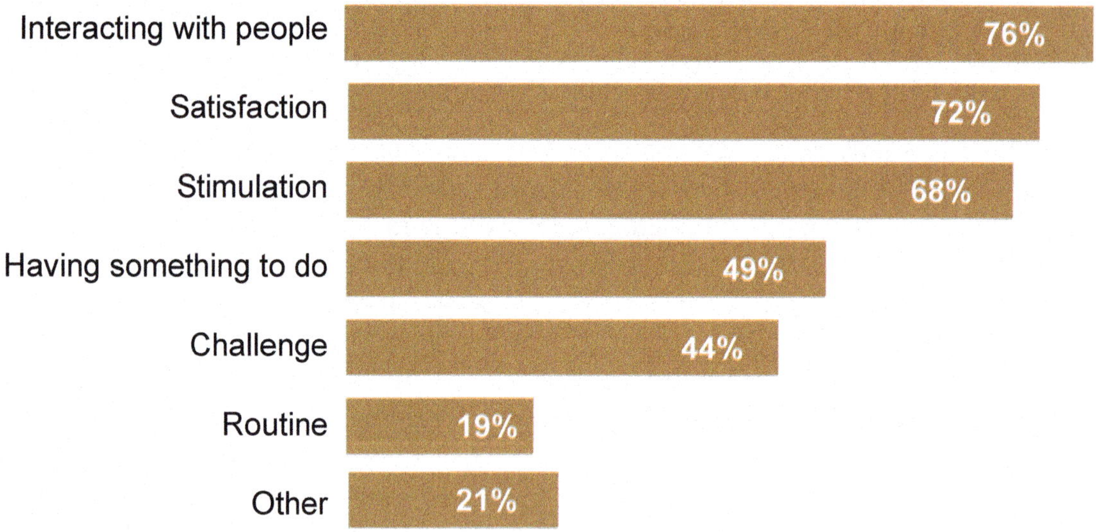

Here are a few comments classified on Table 4-2, as 'other' reasons for working in re-tirement.

I was asked to be on the faculty at our local Hygiene progam.

I work as the Executive Director of my component dental society partly because no one else would do it.

Giving back to the profession by teaching.

Feeling relevant and having a purpose and making a difference.

If I didn't need the money I would start a rock band and record albums.

After 42 years I'm still working 36 hours per week and enjoying it. Health is great and I take time off when ever I want. Solo practice with no plans of retirement.

Giving back to the younger generation of dentists my experience and knowl-edge.

Help transition the practice to the new buyer.

My practice was one of "friends treating friends".

I wanted to periodically see my friends.

Teaching prosthodontics at a dental school is the best form of retirement from private practice.

Helped other dentists keeping their offices staffed so they could pursue vacations and needed surgeries.

I love dentistry and have been able to do it when I want, where I want, and on whom I want. It keeps me connected with the profession and colleagues. It allows me to use my lifetime of skills for the benefit of others. Only dentists can do dentistry, and it is a service appreciated by everyone on the planet.

Postponing Re-tirement

Here is something to ponder. One would assume that working in re-tirement was a function of economic conditions. As conditions worsened, more people would be likely to work in re-tirement. Several research studies carried out after the economic meltdown of 2008, identified a high percentage of workers planning to postpone their re-tirement. For example, the Transamerica Retirement Survey in 2012 found that 60% of the respondents over age 60, plan to work full or part-time when they retire. [(1)] A survey by the Employee Benefit Research Institute put this figure at 70% [(2)], while a study by SunAmerica found that 65% want to include some type of work in retirement.[(3)] A Canadian survey in 2012 found that 53% of people in their 50's plan to work in retirement (CIBC Retirement Survey).[(4)]

If we look at this same issue before the economic meltdown, we are in for a bit of a surprise. In 2004 one study found that 75% of older workers said that it's at least likely that they will work for pay after they retire,[(5)] and in 2006, another study reported that 77% expect to work for pay after they retire.[(6)] We can add to this the fact that 53% of your re-tirement mentors actually worked for a salary since re-tiring There must be something more to postponing re-tirement than meets the eye.

The answer lies partially in the reasons for wanting to postpone re-tirement. When the subjects of the 2004 study were asked why they wanted to work in re-tirement, they focused mainly on non-financial issues including staying mentally alert (93%), to feel useful (74%), and for social interaction (86%). The least mentioned reason was that they needed the money (44%). The 2006 study reported that most wanted to work "because they'll want to, not because they'll have to."

Financial conditions definitely exerted influence on the decision to work in re-tirement since 2008. However, the non-financial reasons also had a major affect. For example, in the TransAmerica 2012 study cited above, 41% planned to work because they enjoyed the work or wanted to stay involved. In the Canadian survey only one third of those who plan to work post retirement said they would do so just for the money and two-thirds – or 67% – saw working either as a way to stay socially active or that they just found work enjoyable and wanted to stay involved in the workforce in some capacity.

It is safe to assume, therefore, that many of your re-tirement mentors found work in re-tirement because they wanted to, not because they had to.

Dave mentioned that he might consider looking for other work when he re-tires so I asked him what type of work he was thinking of.

"I haven't made up my mind on this yet," he replied.

"If you recall, last week when we talked I mentioned that under the old definition where retirement without the dash was defined as withdrawal from work, if somebody went back to work they were referred to as semi-retired, which I guess means 'sort-of-retired' or 'half-retired'. By defining re-tirement as a career earned by and following work, working in re-tirement does not require a special label. In fact, today it is quite common."

Even though Dave had not made up his mind about working, I wanted to give him something to think about - to help him make up his mind. I told the others that most of what I had to say about working also applied to non-work activities.

Taking the Easy Way Out

"First of all, Dave," I said, "like most re-tirement issues, I can't tell you what to do. For some people working in re-tirement is the best course of action, and it can be the opposite for others.

"Having said that, I highly recommend as part of the decision process you ask yourself a very important question. You should try to be honest with your answer. The question is, in your desire to replace satisfactions lost from work, are you taking the easy way out by going back to work?"

"What do you mean?" he responded.

"Well, have you given serious thought to why you are thinking about going back to work when you re-tire?"

"Sure I have," he replied.

"My skills are fairly marketable, but something in me is pushing me to think about doing something completely different. However, I don't know what it could be. Besides, Diane doesn't want me hanging around the house. I have to find something to do when I re-tire."

"That sounds like good reasoning," I said.

I asked the others if they could think of other benefits to working in re-tirement.

"It gives you the opportunity to be with other people and it can be stimulating," suggested Diane.

"Absolutely," I replied. "We talked about this earlier. Besides money, work can satisfy many needs including friendships, routine, getting out of the house, challenge, stimulation, identity, and so on. Some people work in re-tirement because they need the money. Others go back to work to satisfy these additional needs. There is nothing wrong with this providing you consider it worthwhile and enjoyable - providing it satisfies your other needs. If it didn't turn out this way, I take back my endorsement.

"Obviously, if a person had to earn extra money it may be necessary to ignore the non-monetary needs to satisfy the need for extra income. So, Dave, before you rush out to look for a job, pause and take stock of your situation. As I am sure you are aware, besides its positive benefits, working can hold some potentially negative consequences."

"I realize that," said Dave. "And that's why I am having a problem deciding."

"Let me tell you about Mark who I met in a workshop. He worked for a government agency and because he had been with the agency most of his working life, he would end up with a good pension when he re-tired. Anyway, during our workshop he talked about his love of history. Apparently, he would have loved to pursue this years ago, but had to give it up to earn a living. When I asked about his re-tirement plans, he said he was going to look for a part-time job.

"I was somewhat surprised because re-tirement would be the perfect time for him to pursue his long lost dream. If not now, when? I didn't know all the details, maybe he had to work, or he may have been afraid to go back to school. Whatever his reason, it seemed as though he was giving up the perfect opportunity to pursue his dream. He may have been taking the easy way out by going back to work.

"The problem is, working in re-tirement is not necessarily a magic panacea. It can have a down side. Although it may satisfy some of your needs, such as earning money, working in re-tirement can impose restrictions and it may not satisfy all your important needs. And as we all know, the key to re-tirement happiness is to satisfy your important needs."

Evaluating Work

To help evaluate if working was Dave's best solution, I told him to look at his Life Goal List and to identify the five most important needs or skills that must be satisfied when he re-tired. I asked him to think about each item, to be honest and to list these items on a separate piece of paper.

When he completed his list I asked, "Did you include money on your list?"

"Yes," he answered.

Then I said, "If you had to identify two items in your top five list that must be part of your re-tirement, would earning money be one of them?"

"Probably not," he replied.

"In that case," I asked, "would you agree that money is not your main motivation for working in re-tirement?"

"I don't know," said Dave. "Right now things look OK, but you never know what will happen in the future. The stock market is unpredictable so of course the financial side is very important."

"I am not denying that," I replied, "but there are many more things to consider when making the decision to re-tire or whether or not to work in re-tirement."

To help him think about this decision more clearly, I suggested that he imagine or think about working for somebody and ask himself if the items on his Needs and Skills List, especially his top five needs, would be met. I acknowledged that this may be difficult now and that he may have to wait until he found a job in re-tirement.

I suggested that he could add additional needs that did not appear on his original Needs and Skills list. These could include things like sleeping in, spending time with Diane, not being tied down, and so on. This exercise would also give him a better idea of what type of activity to look for. For example, if stimulation or spending more time with Diane were high on his list of priorities, he should bear this in mind when deciding about working in re-tirement.

"If you start to work," I continued, "and if things are not going well, don't forget that you have an ace up your sleeve. Consider this as one-step in your re-tirement career. You have the tools to get you to the next step. Who knows, you may discover an idea that may never have occurred to you had you not started to work. So even if it doesn't work out, you may be able to benefit from it."

Postponing or Working in Re-tirement

If you feel that you have to make up a re-tirement shortfall by continuing to earn money, is it preferable to postpone or work in re-tirement? You could argue that this difference is semantic because if you are working in re-tirement you have postponed your re-tirement, and vice-versa. However, for our purposes they are quite different. The former refers to retaining the status quo, continuing with your current job or work, while the latter refers to re-tiring and finding some way to earn extra income in re-tirement like finding a full-time or part-time job, or creating your own money making venture. To return to the question above, the choice between postponing or working in re-tirement depends on if you can stay where you are, how much of a financial shortfall you need to make up, and where you can satisfy more of your needs.

Obviously if you cannot stay where you are, for example if you lose your job, the decision has been made for you and if necessary you will have to increase your income through another source. The next consideration, how much of a financial shortfall you need to make up, is very important. If, for example, you only have to make up a small portion of your re-tirement income, it may not be necessary to postpone your re-tirement, especially if your work does not satisfy your main needs. At the same time, if you decide to look for work in re-tirement, you might consider part-time rather than full-time work.

There is absolutely nothing wrong with postponing or working in re-tirement providing it enables you to meet your Life Goal. In fact, the extra income is a bonus. However, if it does not allow you to satisfy your needs, and if you do not absolutely have to earn extra money, it's time to reconsider your options. That may not necessarily mean giving up the idea of working; it might mean working for you rather than for others. Even though this option may not be for everyone, we can look at it in more detail. This means that in looking for work you have to be creative and open to new ideas and opportunities.

If you are seeking a job or planning to start a business venture after re-tirement, you will need a plan of action that involves taking a series of steps. Depending on how marketable your skills are, the key to finding a job is to prepare yourself. Most dentists have marketable skills that can be used. Even if you have a marketable skill, this should not prevent you from trying something new. Often you can transfer your skills to other areas. Learning a new skill does not diminish with age. All you need is the desire and a little research to select those that appeal to you and have the highest marketability. Check with your local school board or college for night classes. You may be surprised at what they are offering. You can also consider taking a course by either correspondence or attending a college or university.

Don't let your age inhibit you when looking for a job. Every reliable survey has shown that older employees are more dedicated, more dependable, more conscientious, and have less absenteeism than younger workers have. They require less supervision, take their jobs more seriously, and have a greater sense of responsibility and loyalty to their employers. Their experience, more acute judgment, and maturity make them more efficient.

Before you apply for a job, imagine doing it and evaluate that job against your Needs and Skills List. If you get the job and it does not turn out to be all that you expected, assess it again to find out what is missing. If it does not meet your main needs and skills, you might consider moving on to something else. Unless you absolutely have to earn money, don't waste your re-tirement doing something you don't enjoy (i.e. that doesn't satisfy your most important needs and skills). Unless it is essential, do not sacrifice other needs to the need for money. If the need for money is not imperative, you might consider looking for a non-monetary activity to satisfy your other important needs. Alternatively, if the need for money is important, and you can't find a job that is worthwhile and enjoyable, you may have to create an activity that earns money. That is what Life Goal Planning is all about.

Create a Money Making Venture

If you cannot find a job in re-tirement, you do not necessarily have to abandon your thoughts about work or earning money. You can focus on creating a money-making venture. The main advantage of this option is that you may be able to satisfy more needs than you would have if you postponed your re-tirement or found another job. If you only have to make up a portion of your re-tirement income, if your current work fails to satisfy your Life Goal needs, or if you cannot postpone your re-tirement, you might consider looking into ways to earn that portion in re-tirement and at the same time, you may be able to satisfy your Life Goal.

Creating a money-making venture can start with the brainstorming exercise, (overview in Chapter 3, details in the Appendix) and you have to start with an idea or an inspiration that will develop and evolve through imagination, insight and experience. Here you are looking for suggestions that satisfy the items on your Life Goal List, but with the added condition that the suggestions satisfy your need for extra money. Start by brainstorming (alone or with a group) some small money making ideas. It would be good to include others in the process as they may come up with an idea that may not occur to you. Do this for a while, and select the suggestion with the most appeal but does not require a major investment. Start to look into it, talk to people, maybe volunteer in that area, and do anything to get more insight into your initial idea. You may learn something about another approach that you were not aware of initially. Be creative, think, ask around, experiment, and learn. Remember, re-tirement is a career and to find a money making venture you have to start somewhere, so keep your eyes and ears tuned to new ideas.

Word of Warning

It goes without saying that if you plan to invest in a business venture when you re-tire, that you do your due diligence and check it out thoroughly. I have met a few re-tirees who were relatively comfortable financially, and because they were bored, bought into a business that eventually failed. I am not privy to the financial issues involved, but it is extremely important that you do not rush into something before checking it out thoroughly. In your desire to 'get back to work,' don't risk your financial reserves because it may be very difficult to make up your losses.

Chapter Summary

- Working in re-tirement is not necessarily a magic panacea. It can have a down side. Although it may satisfy some of your needs, it can impose restrictions and it may not satisfy all your important needs.
- You can use your Life Goal List to evaluate whether a particular work activity will satisfy your non-financial needs, and if not, to help find an alternative that may or may not include remuneration.
- 53% of your re-tirement mentors worked for a salary since re-tiring.
- Only 12% found work in re-tirement strictly for the money, suggesting that for many dentists working in re-tirement usually serves as a vehicle to replace non-monetary satisfactions lost from work.
- The top 5 reasons for working in re-tirement included satisfaction, mixing with people, stimulation, having something to do, and challenge.

TIME
MONEY

5

(MONEY) CAN'T BUY ME LOVE

(The Beatles, 1964)

INTEGRATE LIFE GOAL & FINANCIAL PLANNING

Life Goal Planning is an integral part of financial planning and it was important for the group to understand this connection. I am not a financial planner; my experience lies with the non-financial side of re-tirement education. Having said that, over the years I have worked closely with many different financial planners and advisors, conducting re-tirement education workshops. It appears to me that financial planning on its own is not re-tirement planning; it is money management planning. I would argue that Life Goal Planning is the missing element that can transform financial planning into re-tirement planning. People spend both time and money in re-tirement, so true re-tirement planning requires both Life Goal and financial planning.

Because of the need to plan for re-tirement, particularly for the lifestyle side, the survey included a few questions on this issue. Only 34% of the respondents received re-tirement planning assistance before they re-tired and based on the information in Table 5-1, it was predominantly financial planning. However, when they were asked what advice they would offer regarding re-tirement planning (Chapter 1), 45% urged you to plan your time. When asked about areas where they could have given more attention in Table 5-2, 51% felt they were fully prepared, and 33% (18% + 15%) emphasized the need for more non-financial planning.

Table 5-1. Re-tirement Planning Content

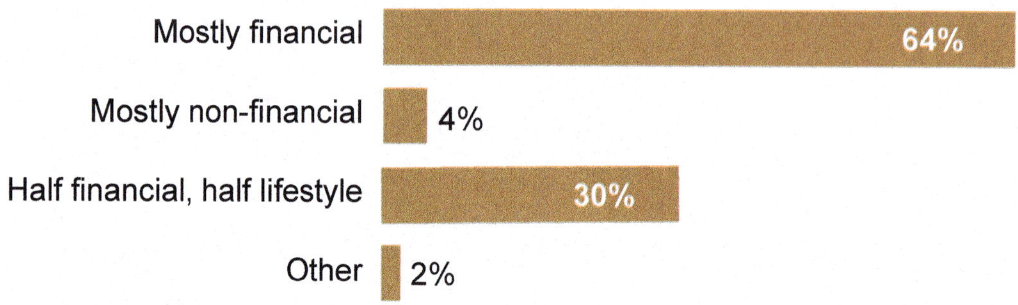

Table 5-2. More Attention Needed

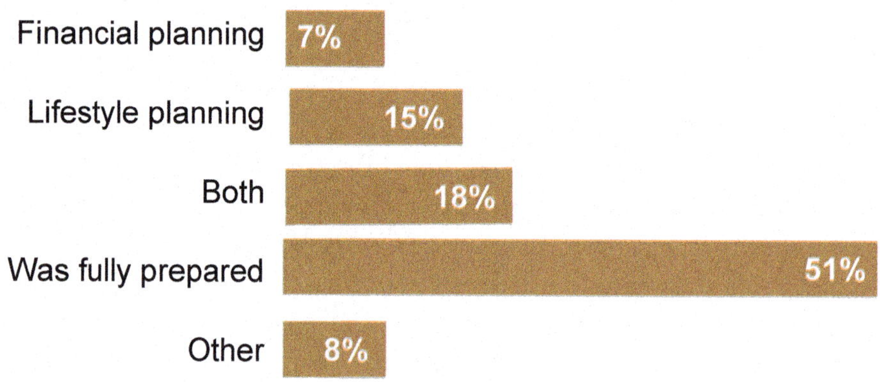

In response to the question of who provided the pre-retirement planning, 81% used the services of a financial planner, 40% self study, 8% the American Dental Association, 8% the Association of Retiring Dentists, and 20% identifed 'Other'.

To explain this to the group, I said, "Let's change the focus a little bit and look at the connection between Life Goal and financial planning."

"But I'm already re-tired," said Les. "It's too late."

"I realize that," I acknowledged. "But the benefits of combining the two can apply anytime before or after re-tirement and they can apply to areas that may surprise you."

"But Dave and I have a financial planner," Diane added. "And he's done a pretty good job considering the ups and downs of the market."

"That's great," I said. "But tell me, when you started with him how did he set up your plan? What I mean is, did he sit down with you to determine a financial goal for re-tirement?"

Dave looked at Diane with a quizzical look on his face and replied, "Yes I think he did."

"Don't you remember," said Diane. "We spent a lot of time with him in the beginning and he asked us a bunch of questions to get an idea of our financial situation."

"How did you establish your financial goal?" I asked.

"I don't remember," said Dave.

"I do," replied Diane. "We told him we wanted to maximize our income and minimize our taxes. But I think he came up with a number based on a percentage of our income."

Establishing a financial goal is central to developing a financial plan - you have to know where you are heading before you can devise a plan to get there. According to the Financial Planning Association, "The financial planning profession exists to help people reach their financial goals and dreams." (www.fpanet.org) Speaking as a non-financial planner observing the financial planning process, most financial planners claim to personalize financial planning but few are truly able to 'walk the talk' because they do not have the tools to follow through. The problem is, most people don't have a clear idea of their 're-tirement dreams' or how they plan to spend their time in re-tirement, which is critical for establishing a financial goal. As I mentioned to Dave earlier, two-thirds of pre-re-tirees I meet in my workshops do not have a concrete plan for re-tirement. Therefore, they or their financial planners have to take an educated guess to identify a financial goal.

Most financial planners estimate a financial goal as somewhere between seventy and eighty percent of the individual's annual salary prior to re-tirement. Surely, this can present problems. First, many people may not have any idea what their future salary will be and the further from re-tirement, the more problematic this becomes. Second, everybody is different. Some people may not need that much in re-tirement, while others may need more. If Dave started to work and earned extra income, he may not need as much as he originally planned for. If it didn't work out, he would need more. Third, financial conditions could change significantly at any time before or after re-tirement and the financial plan should be able to account for these differences. This is where Life Goal Planning comes in.

"One way to understand how the two forms of planning interact and influence each other is to look at planning a vacation. In the process of planning a vacation one of the most important things you have to determine in advance is how much it is going to cost. To figure this out you have to decide..." I wrote the words on a sheet of paper.

Figure 5-1

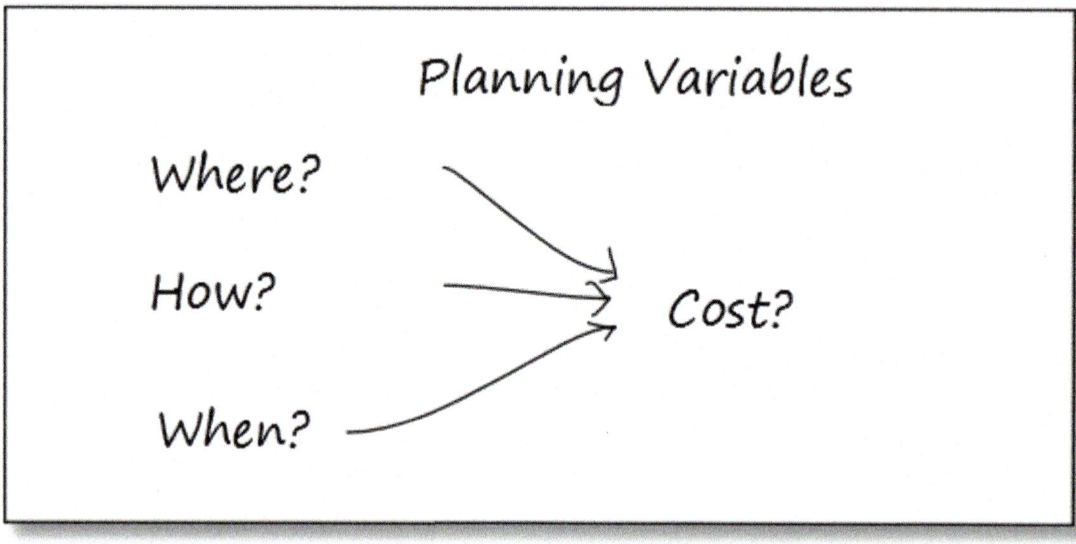

"Where you are going, how you will get there, and when you will leave. Now let's suppose you know the where, how, and when of your vacation, and you determine the cost and decide that given your current financial situation, it is too expensive. You can still take a vacation providing you adjust some of the other variables. For example, to adjust the where variable, you can go to a less expensive destination or find a less expensive hotel. To adjust the how variable you can go on a camping trip, or you can travel during low season to adjust the when variable. If these options are not acceptable or you don't want to make any changes, you can postpone your vacation to save more money until you can afford the vacation you want.

"Financial planning for re-tirement should involve the same variables and a similar process. So before you establish your financial goal or calculate how much your re-tirement will cost, you have to determine the where, how, and when of re-tirement. Let's start with the first variable; where you are going. As we discussed, your objective or destination is to satisfy your needs and skills, especially those lost from work. You know how to identify these items, so you should be able to identify your destination with some degree of accuracy. Second, how will you get there? This includes the plans you have made to reach your destination. You have learned how to evaluate and perhaps improve on a plan, and how to come up with new plans. If you include when you plan to re-tire, and your risk level, you have the core information you need to develop a personalized plan to estimate your future financial needs or goals.

"Another way to look at this connection is both Life Goal and financial planning share the same objective. They both involve helping you plan for a life after work that will be worthwhile and enjoyable. The difference is financial planning focuses on how to finance or fund a future lifestyle, while Life Goal Planning focuses on how to find a future lifestyle - but not just any lifestyle, one that will enable you to replace satisfactions lost from work. The connection is in the two key words 'finance' and 'find'. Planning how to get there, and making corrections along the way, starts by knowing where you are heading.

"Let's look at a different scenario, I continued. "Suppose you re-tire or are re-tired and your financial situation changes and you find you have a financial shortfall."

Les seemed to perk up at this point, so I explained, "Suppose you determine where, how, and when you are going to re-tire and you discover that your financial situation will not support your intended re-tirement lifestyle. You have an imbalance with a financial shortfall. You know how you would like to spend your time in re-tirement but your financial situation won't support your plans. To continue with the vacation analogy, after you determine the where, how, and when of re-tirement and calculate the cost, if you decide you can't afford to re-tire, to correct this situation, if you look strictly for a financial solution you can work longer, sell assets, or invest for a higher return. If you don't want to or can't adjust the financial domain, there is another option; you can adjust some - but not all - of the lifestyle variables. You can adjust the 'when' variable or postpone re-tirement, or the 'how' variable and find re-tirement activities that satisfy the same needs but cost less. Remember, the key to re-tirement happiness is to satisfy your needs, and often you can satisfy the same need or skill by a different activity. The one variable that remains constant regardless of your financial circumstances is your 'where' variable - your Life Goal, or the needs and skills you hope to satisfy in re-tirement."

My concern with the issue is on a broader level looking at how to satisfy your needs through different re-tirement plans that cost less. You can apply the Life Goal Planning techniques outlined in Chapter 3, only here you will be looking for activities that satisfy the items on your Life Goal List with the added condition or need that the suggested activities are less costly. An example might help here. Suppose you include travel as part of your re-tirement plans but realize now that you cannot afford it. Start by identifying your needs that will be met through this activity. Look at your Life Goal List, select another column, and identify those items that you will meet through travel, and then brainstorm an alternative, alone or with others, that could satisfy those needs along with the additional need of costing less.

Broaden your thinking and remember you can often meet the same need through a different activity. So besides thinking about ways to travel more economically, for example, driving instead of flying, renting a mobile home instead of a condo, traveling by freighter instead of a cruse ship, a home swap for an extended stay, try to come up with some creative alternatives. I know a lawyer who re-tired and became a travel writer for a local publication. He isn't paid for his writing but he and his wife have taken advantage of free travel provided by various hotels, restaurants, and cruise lines. Try to stretch your imagination and be creative. Maybe you can find a non-travel, hence less expensive alternative that satisfies many of the same needs. Life Goal Planning can be your ace in the hole. You have the tools to adjust the lifestyle dimension and you do not have to rely solely on the financial dimension for your re-tirement happiness.

Volunteering

To change the subject somewhat, I asked them if they were involved with voluntary or charitable organizations. Janice mentioned that she was part of an adult literacy program and went on to tell us the benefits of her volunteer work.

Les then said, "Janice keeps telling me that I should join the program, but the truth is, I am just not interested. I feel a bit guilty about that, especially since I have so much free time on my hands."

I asked Dave and Diane if they were ever involved in volunteer work and they both said that they were not. Then I said, "When we did our survey among retired dentists, 57% mentioned that they pursued some type of volunteer or charitable activity. It's often looked on as the ideal re-tirement activity that could replace satisfactions lost from work without the constraints of a paid job and can be viewed as a win-win situation, with the added benefit of giving back to society, and benefiting the recipients."

In response to Les's comments about feeling guilty, I wanted to clarify a few issues and said, "We found a curious situation among the people in our survey who volunteered. When we asked if they volunteered before they re-tired, 84% were involved with these types of activities before re-tirement.

"This suggests that those people who were inclined to volunteer in re-tirement were also more likely to pursue these activities before they re-tired. In other words, volunteering is not for everyone and if you are not so inclined, you need not feel guilty."

"Well, I suppose you are right," replied Les, "but I still wish I could find something to fill my time."

"Another issue to think about," I said, "is to be aware of the possibility of rejection even in a volunteer situation." It told them about George, from my workshop, who sold his business and in thinking about what he could do in re-tirement, discovered a government agency that paired re-tired business people with young entrepreneurs. He had developed a very successful business and was quite excited about the prospect of sharing his 'street smarts'. By the way, he had never volunteered before. When he contacted the agency, he was told that they had too many re-tired business people and not enough interested entrepreneurs. Although this was not a personal rejection, in essence he was told that he was not needed. George felt rejected and deflated. Nevertheless, and this is hypothetical, he could have learned something from this experience. For example, after learning that the agency did not have enough entrepreneurs signed up, he could have approached the agency and volunteered to find entrepreneurs; he still had many business contacts from the past. On the other hand, he could have talked to others who felt like him and together they may be able to develop some alternative method to help others. Once the creative juices begin to flow, opportunities are endless.

Here is a break down of the types of volunteer activities pursued by your re-tirement mentors, followd by a few examples on 'Other'volunteer opoportunities.

Table 5-3. Type of Volunteer Activities

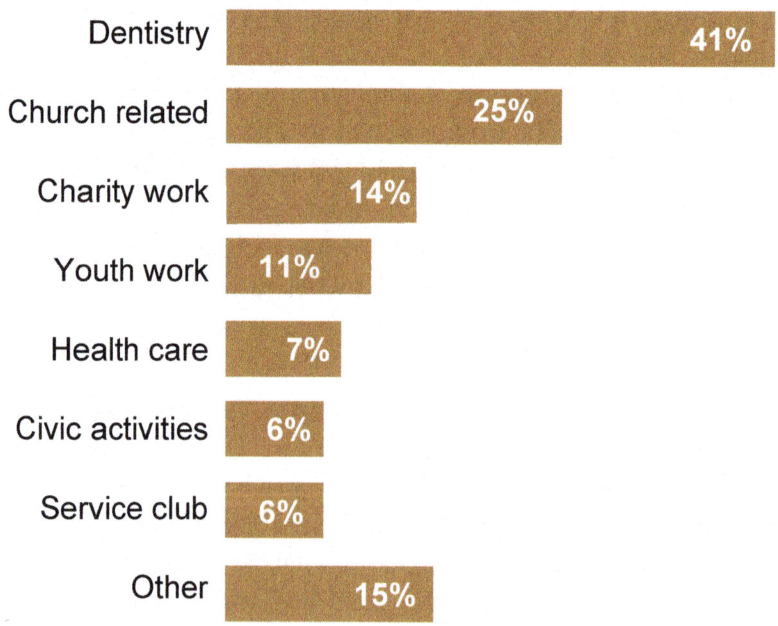

Coaching, teaching mathematics and tutoring

Court appointed special advocacy

Everything from starting our own Charitable Foundation that is now nationwide, to photographing......athletics when the teams travel. Fortunately, I have been photographing in the medical tents at the finish line for the Boston Marathon for the past ten years.

Figure skating judge

Genesee Health Plan, Alumni Association, mentor

Hobby is woodturning- I serve as mentor to young men who seek their way in life and I donate works of art for various charities

Holocaust center

I teach calligraphy and help with mission type projects

In charge of fitness area of community center

Love music. Have been a DJ at a public radio station

On committee to put on a charity/memorial golf tournament to honor a friend's deceased son (killed in a car accident)

Refugee resettlement. Bee keeping mentor

Special Olympics

United States Coast Guard Auxillary

Volunteer as a guide

Volunteer at Back Bay National Wildlife Reserve

Volunteer for KART, a horseback riding therapy group for handicapped persons, River Water Tester for the Sassafrass River in Maryland, Member of the Planning and Zoning Commission for our Town, Councilman for our Town

Working with non-kill animal shelter for dogs and cats.

As you can see by the list above, there are many volunteer opportunities beyond the traditional health care situations, and there are several Web sites devoted to matching volunteers with agencies. A cursory look at one site listed volunteer opportunities for an art and wine reception coordinator, web site designers, grant writers, theatrical groups, media and communication internships, and the list goes on.

It was getting late and it was time to wrap things up. So I told them that I had covered the issues that I wanted to present and that hopefully I gave them an idea of how the process works. I encouraged them to redo the exercises on their own or with a group.

"We definitely will go through it again," said Les.

"So will we," said Dave.

"Glad to hear it," I said.

I thanked them for being such an attentive group and got up to leave. They thanked me and once again assured me that they would complete the exercises as soon as possible.

As I got up to leave, Diane asked if my wife and I were going to attend the block party. I told her we were planning to attend and that we would see her and Dave at the party. As I left, they were discussing inviting another couple to join them in a few days to go through the workshop in more detail.

Chapter Summary

- You have two re-tirement goals, a 'Financial Goal' and a 'Life Goal' and each requires different planning methods. Your financial goal is to finance your re-tirement, and your Life Goal is to satisfy your personal needs in re-tirement. The link between these goals lies in the type of activities you pursue; you want to find activities that will satisfy your needs and that you can afford.
- Planning for re-tirement starts by having some idea of how much it will cost - a financial goal. First you have to identify the needs and skills you want to satisfy in re-tirement (your re-tirement Life Goal), and the activities you plan to pursue to satisfy your re-tirement Life Goal. Then if you factor in your re-tirement date, you can develop a personalized financial plan.
- If you have a financial shortfall at re-tirement, besides considering changes in the financial domain, Life Goal Planning will enable you to create alternative and possibly less costly activities in the non-financial domain that will satisfy your needs lost from work.
- The Life Goal Planning Exercises in Part 3, include a section to summarize your findings that can be shared with a financial planner to incorporate with your financial plan.
- Volunteering can be viewed as a win-win situation that can replace many satisfactions formerly met by work with the added benefit of giving back to society.
- 57% of your re-tirement mentors pursued volunteer activities and 41% of the volunteer activities related directly to dentistry. In contrast, 90% of work activities in re-tirement related to dentistry (See Chapter 4).
- 84% were involved with these types of activities before re-tirement, suggesting that those people who were inclined to volunteer in re-tirement were more likely to pursue these activities before they re-tired.
- Volunteering is not for everyone and if you are not so inclined, you need not feel guilty.

CHANGE
SAME

6

DID YOU EVER HAVE TO MAKE UP YOUR MIND?

(The Lovin' Spoonful, 1965)

THE DECISION TO RE-TIRE

Every summer the people who live in our neighborhood get together for a block party. It's an informal potluck affair and various families contribute drinks and food. This tradition has been going on for several years, it always includes a collection of adults, kids, and dogs, and I often see people I have not seen since last summer's party. This year the party took place a few weeks after my session with Dave and Diane and I was curious to see if they continued with the program on their own and if it was helping Dave with his re-tirement plans.

When we arrived at the party, I waved at Dave and Diane who were speaking to a few other people. My wife spotted and joined an old friend and I made my way over to join Dave and Diane.

Diane was signaling for me to join them and as I approached, I heard him say, "Here's the guy I was telling you about. I'll introduce you."

Dave introduced me to Lynn who recently moved into the neighborhood and explained that they were talking about the session at his house a few weeks ago. He also introduced Craig who was re-tired.

After the introductions, Lynn said, "Dave tells me that you help people plan for re-tirement."

"Well, yes," I replied. "I conduct workshops and I focus on the non-financial side of re-tirement."

"That's interesting," said Lynn.

Dave interjected and said, "We have been talking about re-tirement and I told them about your new way of looking at re-tirement, with a dash. It's funny, but lately I have spoken to quite a few people who are starting to think about it."

"Let's face it," I said. "Re-tirement is becoming a fact of life for people our age. Suddenly it's no longer far off in the future. Now, it's a reality."

I asked Craig what he did before re-tirement. He said he was in the insurance business and that he re-tired a few years ago.

"Well," I asked, "how is re-tirement treating you?"

"It's great," he replied.

"He's a politician," said Diane. "Don't you recognize him? He's a City politician."

"I knew your name sounded familiar," I said. "How did you get into politics?"

"I have been interested in politics for many years and I like to be involved. When I re-tired I thought, what the heck, why not go for it. I love the job actually."

Lynn had a thoughtful look on her face and said, "If I had a million dollars in the bank, I'd re-tire tomorrow."

I had come across this type of thinking before so I said to Lynn, "I once met a guy who said the exact same thing. I think he was willing to re-tire for less, but that was some time ago and with inflation today he may well say one million. The point is, as we talked I got the impression that his thoughts on re-tiring ran much deeper than an amount of money in the bank."

To expand on this issue, I said, "Let me ask you a couple of questions, Lynn. Suppose you had a million dollars in the bank."

"That would be nice," she replied.

"Would you really re-tire?"

She thought about her answer and with a slight grin on her face she said, "I really don't know."

"Fair enough," I said. "The next question is, if you had a million dollars in the bank and after meeting me would you say to me, if only I had two million dollars in the bank I would re-tire tomorrow?"

She smiled and said, "That's a good question. The truth is, I sort of have a love/hate thing with my job, and re-tirement may be an option."

"When can you re-tire?" I asked.

"I'm a lawyer and with my firm I can re-tire whenever I want. Some people in our firm who should have re-tired years ago, and maybe I am one of them. Nevertheless,

I'm still hanging in and plodding away. For me, it's a tough decision to make. What happens if I don't like it?"

Lynn asked me at what age most people re-tire and I told her that there is no simple answer to that question. Statistically people are re-tiring younger, but statistics mean nothing. Everybody's conditions are different. "For some people the decision is made for them by the rules set out in their pension formula or the workplace, although mandatory retirement is fast becoming a thing of the past, or by health considerations. For people who have some control over when they can re-tire, it can be a difficult decision because so many factors can come into play.

I asked Lynn if she had any plans for re-tirement.

"The problem is," she replied, "I could re-tire but I like my work. I mean it has its problems, but all in all I like going to work."

"Then why are you thinking about re-tiring?" I asked. "If you don't have to re-tire and if you enjoy your work, there is nothing wrong with staying where you are."

"I realize that," said Lynn. "But a few of my friends have re-tired and I guess it's kind of infectious. One of my closest friends re-tired last year and she is having a great time. In fact, I hardly get a chance to see her anymore. And look at Craig; he's having the time of his life."

Craig beamed in agreement, so I asked him how he made the decision to re-tire.

"I can't remember, exactly," he replied. "But as I said, I have always been interested in politics and quite frankly, I have been in insurance for so long that I was definitely in need of a change. So, it sort of came naturally. One day I just sat down and said to myself, if not now, when? I guess I am lucky. In a way, the decision was not hard to make."

I turned to Lynn and said, "Lynn, to get back to your comment about having enough money to re-tire, I have spoken to many people who are in a similar situation. In fact, a few weeks ago Dave and I talked about this issue. If you are thinking about when to re-tire, I can't make the decision for you but I can give you some things to think about."

"I would really appreciate that," said Lynn.

We sat down and I said, "Let's put re-tirement aside for a moment. Say you had another decision to make, such as you want to buy a new car. How would you decide on which car was best for you?"

"I would test-drive a few cars to see which one I preferred," said Dave.

"Suppose you still couldn't decide after a test drive. What else could you do to help with this decision?"

"You could read consumer reports," said Lynn. "Or talk to people who owned each car to get their impressions. Also, you could look at the resale values and safety reports."

"In other words," I said, "you should do your homework. You should gather, compare, and weigh the relevant information. Well, you can apply the same process of gathering, comparing, and weighing the relevant information, to the decision to re-tire.

"The first step," I said, "is to do your homework. You have to gather the relevant information and look at the various factors that can bear on this decision."

I addressed all of them and asked, "What information should you gather in making the decision to re-tire. What factors can come into play?"

Lynn said, "Let me think. I haven't thought about this before. I suppose health can be important. If you are having health problems, you might want to re-tire. And of course money is important."

"Yes, money and health can influence the decision to re-tire," I replied. "But can you think of anything else?"

"If you didn't like your work you might be anxious to re-tire," said Craig.

"That can be very important," I said. "We could also include family considerations, and the timing of a spouse's re-tirement. These can influence the decision for some people. In fact there are three main factors to consider in the decision to re-tire, other factors include health, timing of a spouse's re-tirement, and so on."

Push and Pull Factors

I looked around for something to write on, reached for a napkin, and wrote the following:

"He loves to write messages," said Dave. "The other day he kept writing messages on his fence."

I let this comment pass, smiled, and said, "To make a rational decision about when to re-tire, you have to gather information on these three factors. Push factors include the things you are happy to give up at work, Pull factors are the things you look forward to in re-tirement, and money is, well, money.

"Let's start with money because the first thing that pops into most people's minds when they think of when to re-tire is whether they will have enough money to re-tire. Like you said, Lynn, if only you had a million dollars you would re-tire tomorrow."

"I was just joking," she replied.

"Well," I said, "most people think this way and money is a very important consideration. In fact, when most people think about re-tirement planning the first and often the only thing they think about is financial planning."

"That's true," said Lynn. "When I thought about re-tiring I only thought about how much I needed to re-tire."

"Having enough money is both a quantitative and qualitative judgment," I explained. "The distinction here is between money expressed as a dollar figure such as I need X dollars to re-tire, and a qualitative entity, and only you can judge when enough is enough. Of course, the problem is if you don't know how you will spend your time in re-tirement, it can be difficult to figure out if you have enough money.

"So, in the context of making the decision to re-tire, besides looking at how much money you need, the quantitative dimension, you also have to ask yourself is: When does the fun begin?"

"Does this question sound familiar?" I asked.

"It sure does," said Craig. "Would you believe that I used to have a T-shirt with that written on it?"

"And I recall seeing bumper stickers with this question," I replied.

"Your answer to this question is the first step in the qualitative approach to the decision to re-tire. Would you agree that the word fun is another way of saying enjoyment? I asked"

"Sure," said Lynn. "They mean the same thing."

"As I outlined to Dave and Diane a few weeks ago, the reason we enjoy any activity before or after re-tirement, is because it satisfies our needs. For example, if you think about why you may be enjoying this block party, you might say it's because it satisfies your need to be in the sunshine, to relax, to meet people, eat potato salad, and as an added surprise bonus, to learn something about re-tirement."

"Sounds reasonable," said Lynn. "But what does a party have to do with re-tirement?"

"They are similar because both will be enjoyable if they satisfy your needs. Therefore, the question 'When will the fun begin?' becomes..." I reached for another napkin.

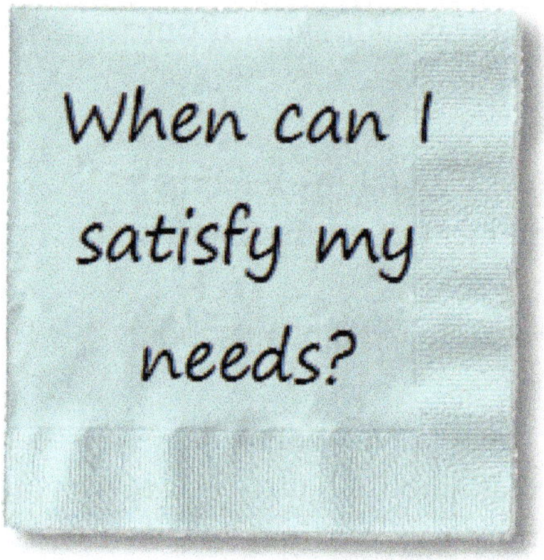

"In fact because of the freedom of re-tirement it can be the perfect opportunity to satisfy your needs."

"It all sounds good," said Lynn, "but I like some parts of my work and I am not so sure about this."

Dave agreed with Lynn on this point.

"The main thing I am suggesting is that in thinking about re-tiring, keep this question in mind", I pointed to my napkin, "because as I mentioned before, money alone will not guarantee re-tirement happiness. And it is very possible that some people use the excuse of not having enough money, where the real problem is they don't know how to replace satisfactions lost from work."

I looked back at my first napkin and said, "The next thing to consider is what I call your Push Factors. As I said, the Push factors include all the things you would be happy to give up or leave behind when you re-tire. These are, figuratively speaking, pushing you into re-tirement. The Pull considerations include the things you are looking forward to in re-tirement, the things that are pulling you into re-tirement.

"Here is what I suggest you do. Start by listing your Push and Pull considerations on a piece of paper. Give this some serious thought and don't be too hasty with this. Then take a hard look at the items in both categories. After comparing your Push and Pull factors, it may become clear which the best option is. Obviously, it would be preferable if you based your decision mainly on Pull factors. If not, re-tiring may be a case of going from the frying pan into the fire. Having said that, eventually, everyone has to re-tire, so you had better get to work to redress the balance between your Push and Pull considerations. If you looked forward to re-tirement, you would be basing your decision mainly on pull factors."

"That sounds like a worthwhile exercise. I will definitely try it," said Lynn.

"Just use this simple formula."

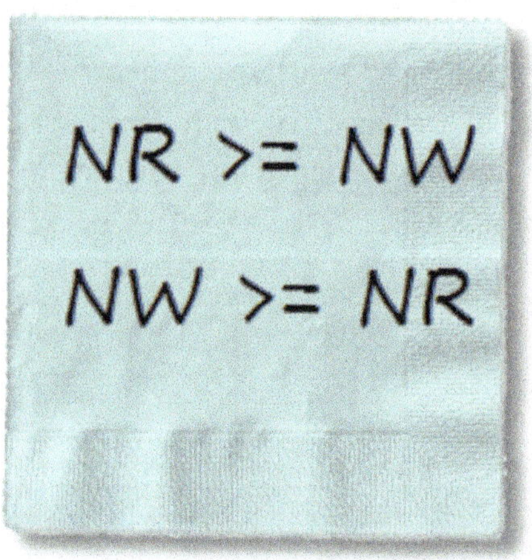

"What does that stand for?" Diane asked.

"It's a shorthand formula," I replied. "NR stands for needs in re-tirement, and NW stands for needs at work. So it reads, you should consider re-tiring when your needs met in re-tirement will be greater than or equal to those currently met at work."

Dave studied my formula and said, "Sounds a bit formal, but that's an interesting way to look at it. How can I figure this out?"

I explained to the others that a few weeks ago I taught Dave and Diane some of the basics of Life Goal Planning and that I based my explanation on that process.

"It's very simple," I replied, "and you're halfway there. When you evaluated your re-tirement plans to see if they would meet your needs and skills, although we only included a few questions, you should have a pretty good idea of those needs and skills that will be met when you re-tire. That takes care of the left side of this equation. Now all you have to do is use another column in your Life Goal sheet to evaluate your needs and skills met by work, and then compare the two columns."

"Now I get it," said Dave."

"So let me ask you again, Lynn. If you had a million dollars in the bank would you re-tire tomorrow?"

Lynn smiled and said, "Not until my Pull factors outweighed my Push factors."

Eighty percent of your re-tirement mentors re-tired by choice, and their reasons for re-tiring included both Pull Factors, things they looked forward to in re-tirement, and Push Factors, things they were quite happy to give up from work (see Table 6-1). Here are a few 'Other' reasons for re-tiring.

Too many new rules/regulations to deal with. I had three employees and did all the paperwork myself.

The practice selling price was at or near the peak and the future projections were going down.

Wasn't busy enough to remain full-time.

I found out a respected colleague of mine helped dentists in transition, I respected him so much I merely asked him if he felt I would able to and if anyone may be interested in purchasing my practice? Several months later, after he had found several interested dentists, things came together so rapidly that I was surprised, thankful, and made the decision with my dear wife who had been my loyal assistant for 30 years, to actually make our decision and follow through with the opportunity!

Table 6-1. Reasons for Re-tiring

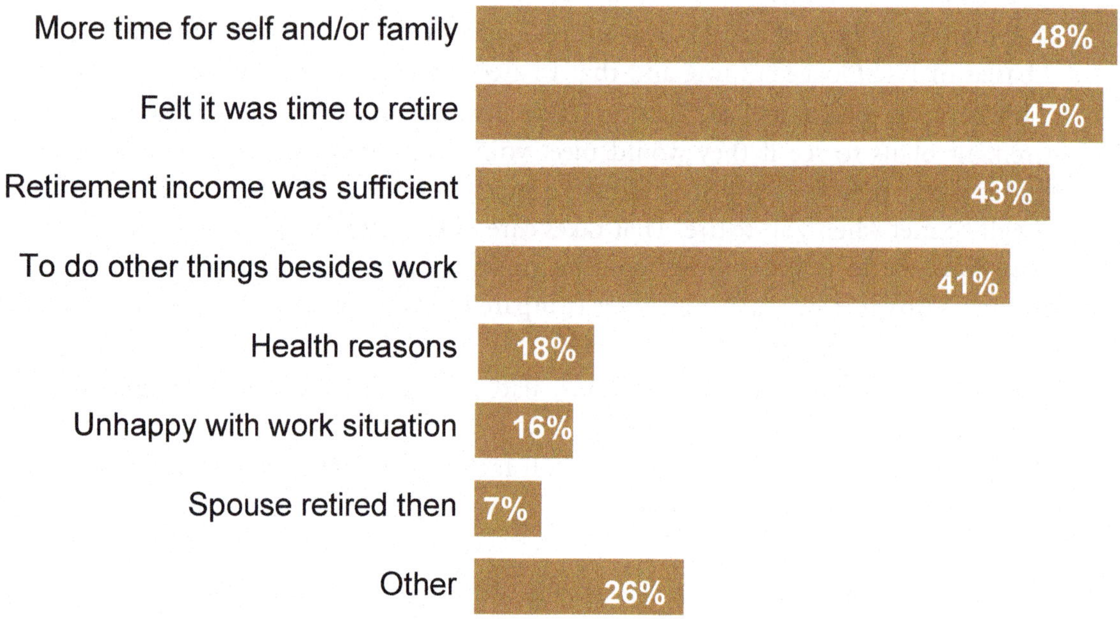

Still working at age 68 and don't plan to "retire" soon. Just acquired another practice and combined with mine. Didn't need it, wanted a new challenge after 42 years. This is my "hobby" and I am good at it.

Teaching opportunity arose and had a willing buyer for practice.

I found the right guy to take over the practice and it was a one time opportunity.

Changed career to primarily teaching.

Spouse died and I lost my desire to continue practicing.

My work load seemed light enough to condense it from four to three days per week. It was an experiment that worked out well.

Wanted to realize the value of the practice. Sold at peak. Wanted smooth transition for patients and staff. Allow new owners to purchase/invest in major new technology. Wanted practice to continue smoothly in case unexpected health issues arose. Concentrate on the things I love about dentistry, and let someone else do the things I didn't like. Have more flexibility and freedom.

Age and Re-tirement

Table 6-2 indicates their ages at re-tirement, and Table 6-3 includes responses to the question, "If you could do it over again would you still retire at the same age?" We see that 56% retired earlier than age 65, and that 57% would retire at the same age if they could do it over again.

Table 6-2. Age at Re-tirement

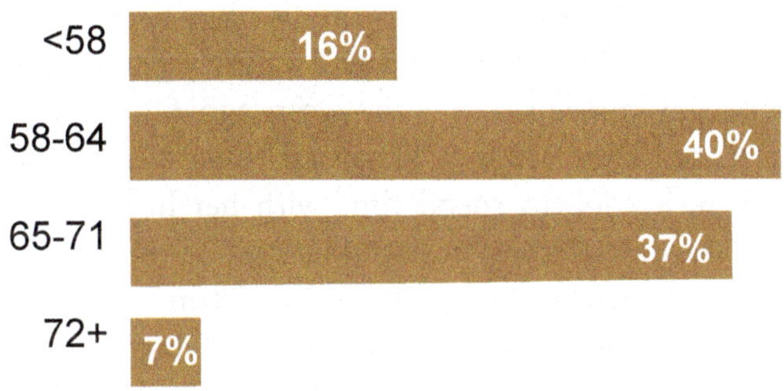

Table 6-3. Re-tire at the Same Age

Spouses Re-tiring Together

"One thing we have been thinking about," said Dave, "is if Diane and I should re-tire at the same time."

"This can complicate things," I said.

I turned to Lynn and Craig and asked them if this was a concern. Lynn said that that she was a single mother and that it was not an issue for her, but she was interested to hear what I had to say about it. Craig said that his wife was still working.

I turned back to Dave and Diane and said, "Some couples prefer to re-tire at the same time, while others do not. This decision involves several factors that deserve serious consideration. From a purely financial perspective, if Diane takes an early re-tirement it might reduce her pension."

"That is not a major problem for us," said Dave.

I told them a story about a couple from one of my workshops who faced this decision. I met Cindy when she was about to re-tire from her job. But she was not looking forward to it because she did not want to spend time with her retired (without the dash) husband. It seems that several years ago, Cindy and her husband both retired at the same time. They had not discussed this in any detail, but she took an early retirement from her job to spend time with her husband. The way Cindy described her situation; the day after her husband retired, he reached into his job jar and decided to paint the house. He woke up at his usual time and they had breakfast together. Then he went outside to paint the house. At 10:00, he took a break and had coffee together. Then he went back to painting the house. At 12:00, they had lunch together, at 2:30 he took a coffee break, and at 4:30 he quit working.

The next day, he followed the same routine. This went on until he finally finished painting the house. At that point Cindy thought, great now we can spend some time together. Well, it didn't work out that way. After painting the house, he rebuilt the garden, and when he ran out of jobs to do at home, he volunteered to help their neighbors fix up their places. Eventually, he ran out of jobs to do.

Then the real trouble began. He started watching TV in the afternoon and hanging around shopping centers because he had nothing to do. Cindy was so frustrated that she went back to her former employer and begged to have her job back. Her former boss rehired her a few years ago and now she was coming up to mandatory retirement and was not looking forward to it.

After relating the story of Cindy and her husband, I did not want them to think this was common. So I said, "This is a rather extreme case and I am not suggesting that it has anything to do with you and Diane. However, it touches on several points that are worth thinking about.

"The first point is, the decision for a couple to re-tire together should not be taken for granted. It requires honest, open dialogue well in advance of re-tirement. Clearly Cindy and her husband had completely different expectations about how they would spend their re-tirement. She expected to spend time with her husband, while he had different ideas. It is also clear that they did not express their feelings about re-tirement before they re-tired. If they had spent time before re-tirement talking about what each thought they would like to do, and if her husband had been honest, as a minimum, Cindy would not have taken an early re-tirement.

"The next consideration is that it appears that Cindy and her husband failed to find worthwhile alternatives after retirement (retired without the dash). Her husband seemingly had plenty to do that he enjoyed when he retired. Nevertheless, eventually he ran out of things to keep him busy.

"Cindy, on the other hand, did not have any plans for retirement and was relying on her husband so they could do things together. Unfortunately, when this failed to materialize, her only consideration was to return to work (she took the easy way out). Like her husband, she did not have anything worthwhile to sustain herself in retirement."

Cindy's husband reminded me of people who soon after re-tirement say they have so much to do, that there just aren't enough hours in the day to do it all. For some people this may be true. Others, I suspect, are filling time with 'busy work.' They lack a Central Life Focus in re-tirement. In addition, when they run out of busy work, problems can set in.

I turned to Dave and Diane and said, "Now is the time for you to start talking about various scenarios for when either or both of you re-tire. Diane, are you thinking of taking an early re-tirement if Dave re-tires soon?"

"I'm not sure what to do," she replied. "We have talked about this, but we haven't made a decision yet. We like to do things together, but this is a major decision. If Dave goes back to work, I might as well stay at work. If he doesn't, then maybe I will re-tire. It depends."

"Here's what I suggest you do," I said. "Both of you should complete the two exercises I mentioned earlier. Evaluate your re-tirement plans and your current work based on your needs and skills. We did this with your re-tirement plans at your house a few weeks ago. This should identify any problems or omissions in either or both of your plans before you re-tire and it will enable you to compare re-tirement with your current work.

"Then think about and list your Push and Pull considerations. If your Push outweighs your Pull list, think about reversing this situation. Think how you can create a re-tirement that would be preferable to being at work. Do these exercises in the context of the broader question, 'When does the fun begin?' If you are honest with yourselves and spend some time with this, the answer you have been searching for just might appear."

"After the session at our house," said Diane, "we both have been looking at our plans. Now we will try these other exercises."

There was a slight pause and Dave said, "There is one more thing that has been bothering me. I hate to admit it but when I think about re-tiring, it's as if I'm getting old. Do you know what I mean? I don't want people to think of me as a senior citizen. It scares me."

"I feel exactly the same way Dave," said Lynn. "I know it's silly, but some things you just can't deny."

"You are touching on a very important topic that is near and dear to my heart," I replied. "I say this because I have spent many years teaching re-tirement education and although this concern is common, it is completely misplaced. The problem is, if you believe that re-tirement is somehow connected to aging or growing old, and this is a common belief, it can have negative consequences. I am not denying that we are getting older. I am simply stating that aging has absolutely nothing to do with re-tirement. The problem is, most people, including many who write books and run courses on retirement, do not understand this issue.

"Before we get into that subject," I said, "one of my immediate needs is to get some more of that delicious potato salad. After I satisfy this need, I will show you a completely different way to look at the issue of aging and re-tirement. I am not trying to sweep this under the carpet hoping it will go away or not be noticed. I want to show you that your concern about growing old and re-tirement is unwarranted and harmful. I'll be right back."

Chapter Summary

- Money alone will not guarantee re-tirement happiness and some people use the excuse of not having enough money, where the real problem is they don't know how to replace satisfactions lost from work.
- To make a rational decision about when to re-tire, you have to gather information on three factors: push factors (the things you are happy to give up at work), pull factors, (the things you look forward to in re-tirement), and money.
- List and compare your Push and Pull considerations. If your financial situation is adequate, you should consider re-tiring when the needs you expect to meet in re-tirement will be greater than or equal to those currently met at work.
- The decision for a couple to re-tire together requires honest, open dialogue well in advance of re-tirement.
- Eighty percent of your re-tirement mentors re-tired by choice, and their top 4 reasons included; more time for self and/or family, felt it was time to retire, retirement income was sufficient, and to do other things besides work.

Happy
Birthday

7

WHEN I'M SIXTY-FOUR

(The Beatles, 1967)

AGING AND RE-TIREMENT

I have spent over 20 years studying, researching, writing about, and teaching the re-tirement experience. This includes many years teaching Social Gerontology (the study of aging) during my university experience, and working with thousands of pre and post-re-tirees through my workshops. Based on this experience I have concluded that in the context of re-tirement, a discussion on aging is both irrelevant and detrimental. It is irrelevant because aging has nothing to do with re-tirement, and it is detrimental because it can reinforce the commonly held misconception that when one re-tires, one is getting old. This may have applied to generations of retirees in the past, but it most certainly does not apply today, especially with people re-tiring so young. So pervasive is the issue that I felt compelled to clear up a few misconceptions.

I returned with a bowl of potato salad, sat down, and said, "When we talked about re-tirement, and aging, you said you were concerned about people thinking of you as old. Unfortunately this feeling is common and it is tied into the traditional image of retirement (without the dash) I discussed earlier with Dave. The problem is most people, including many who write books and run courses on retirement, make this connection. The reason they make the connection is twofold - it has always been part of the thinking about retirement (without the dash), and coincidently, we tend to be older when we re-tire."

The aging process begins at birth. It is common, however, to use the term aging to refer to growing older. It is also common to make the connection between aging in the context of growing older, and re-tirement. In fact one dictionary defines retire as "to withdraw from office, business, or active life, usually because of age (dictionary.com). The structure of private and public pension schemes reinforces this connection. Typically, people re-tire when they are eligible to receive a full pension, and the timing of this is according to age (or some formula taking into account years of service and age). The reason age, rather than say performance, is the determining factor, is because of convenience and tradition. To my mind, it is wrong to base the point of re-tirement primarily on age. Having said that, if we must use age to expedite re-tirement and calculate pension rates, we must not assume a relation between re-tirement and aging or getting old. If you believe this, you are guilty of what I call the 'ageist's self-fulfilling prophecy'. The heart of the matter is wrapped up in the concept called the self-fulfilling prophecy."

Originally conceptualized by Robert Merton in the 1950's, the self-fulfilling prophecy occurs when a false definition of the situation evokes a new behavior, which makes the original false conception come true. In plain English, if we believe something strongly, even if it isn't accurate, we tend to act in ways that are consistent with that expectation. Chapter 1 included an example of the salesman and the missing jack. I recently came across another example from Groucho Marx, the comedian, through a transcript from a recently rediscovered radio show, which aired in 1933. Groucho Marx, Attorney at Law, is speaking to his secretary, about mailing a letter.

It's just a note to my friend, Steve Granach, asking for a loan...but he's probably got his own troubles. I hardly think he can spare it. And even if he had it, I think he'd be a little reluctant to lend me the dough. He's kind of tight that way. Why, I don't think he'd let me have it if I was going hungry. In fact, that guy wouldn't give me a nickel if I were starving. And he calls himself a friend...the cheap swine. I'll show him where to get off. Take a letter to that snake and tell him I wouldn't touch his money. And if he ever comes near this office again, I'll break every bone in his body.

This is another excellent example of a self-fulfilling prophecy. In a few lines, Groucho talked himself into believing that his friend would not lend him any money. He defined the situation as one where even if his friend delivered the money personally, he still wouldn't take it. In fact, he would break every bone in his body!

The self-fulfilling prophecy closely relates to the definition of the situation described earlier. The salesman in Chapter 1, and Groucho Marx above, defined their situations (needing a jack and asking for a loan) in such a way that they no longer wanted the jack or the loan.

After briefly describing the self-fulfilling prophecy to the group, I said, "The same situation can take place with respect to aging and re-tirement. For example, I met a person in my workshop who truly believed that he would not live very long after he re-tired. This was extreme thinking and obviously, I was quite surprised to hear him say this, so I asked how long his parents lived. His mother was 82 and was still alive. His father lived to be over 80. Clearly, there was no biological reason for his belief. But the problem was, he so firmly held on to this belief that he may help to bring it about."

Ageist Self-Fulfilling Prophecy

I explained that this man was guilty of what I call the *Ageist Self-fulfilling Prophecy*. An ageist is to older people as a racist is to certain ethnic groups, and a sexist is to women. Ageism implies prejudice or discrimination against or negative attitudes toward people based on their age. For our purposes, the Ageist Self-fulfilling Prophecy simply means that if you believe that when you re-tire you will be old, or that others will think of you that way, you may look for signs to prove or validate your belief. Moreover, if you look hard enough, you will find them even if you have to create them.

To give an example that they could relate to I asked, "Do any of you know of someone who passed away soon after re-tirement?"

A solemn hush fell over the group. This is a serious matter. After all, these people are about to re-tire and the implications behind this thought are scary.

Diane said to Dave, "What about Alex? Didn't he die about a year after he re-tired?"

"Yes, he did," Dave replied, somewhat reluctantly. "And he wasn't that much older than me. It makes you wonder."

With a somber face I replied, "Terrible isn't it?" I paused to let this thought sink in.

Then I said, "Now let me ask, does anyone know someone who recently re-tired and who is still alive?"

It took a few seconds for this thought to register and when it did, the tone changed from gloom to laughter and relief.

"Our mind does funny things," I said. "If we hear of someone who dies soon after re-tirement, this sticks in our mind. We think re-tirement killed him or her. However, we don't think about the millions of people who may actually live longer because they re-tired. In addition, there is no way to test if Alex would still be alive if he did not re-tire. Once somebody re-tires and dies, you can't bring him or her back to see if they would live longer by not re-tiring. Yet if we hear about someone dying soon after re-tirement, the ageist self-fulfilling prophecy leads us to falsely believe that re-tirement killed him."

I have come across several statements to this effect. For example, "those who make no plans for their retirement years receive on average just 13 Social Security benefit checks, and that seven out of 10 of them die within two years.[1] My response to these statistics can be summarized in a single word; "Hogwash." If we were to look deeper, the only way to determine if the statement is true, that people who had no plans for retirement died within two years of retirement, would be to ask them if they had plans. The problem is, they will have died so we can't ask them. Furthermore, if 70% die within two years, how can we prove that the 30% who live beyond two years of retirement had made plans? Finally, having plans means nothing. The quality of those plans is what counts. Of course, the research did not report this. Be careful interpreting statistics.

Memory and Aging

Another common example of the Ageist's Self Fulfilling Prophecy is memory loss. To emphasize this I said, "I have to admit that I know of a sign of aging that most people experience. Let me ask you another question. Do you find that as you get older, and I am not denying that we are getting older, that you are starting to forget things, like people's names, or where you left your keys?"

"Would you repeat the question," said Craig. "I forget what you were asking."

They all laughed at his comment but I suspect deep down it was a nervous laugh and that they could relate to this problem.

To respond to Craig, I started to repeat my question, stopped and said, "Seriously, if you find that you are starting to forget things, is it logical to conclude that you are getting old?"

There was silence, so I went on to say, "I have some good news and some bad news. The bad news is if you believe that forgetting things is a sign of your age, you are a victim of the Ageist Self-fulfilling Prophecy. The good news is, forgetting things as you get older is not necessarily a result of your age."

"What else could it be?" asked Lynn.

"I will explain that in a minute" I replied.

"I admit that as people get older there is one very important thing they start to forget. I am not talking about forgetting where you put your car keys or a person's name. These are minor compared to what I am referring to."

I went on to ask, "Can anybody tell me, what the most significant thing that people forget as they get older is?"

There was a pause and then Diane said jokingly, "I can think of plenty of things but I don't think Dave wants it aired in public."

"I think forgetting a person's name is pretty significant," said Lynn.

"It's only significant if you see it as a sign of aging," I said. "Besides, not everyone starts to forget people's names as they get older and in a moment I will show you that it is not necessarily a sign of aging."

Again I asked them what people forget as they get older, and again, I did not get a response. Therefore, I answered my own question. "The most important thing that people forget as they get older is that they used to forget things when they were younger."

I paused to let this sink in.

"And more importantly," I continued, "when you were 22 and forgot something you never construed that as a sign of being young. You probably thought, I had too much on my mind, or I will think of it eventually, or I should work at remembering those things, or you just accepted the fact that you had a bad memory.

"But now when you forget things you interpret it as a sign of aging. Secretly at the back of your mind you think, oh my God, I must be getting senile, or have Alzheimer's disease.

"This is the natural conclusion of false logic (or a false definition of the situation). If you start with the assumption that old people forget things and that re-tirees are old, and you start to forget things, the logical conclusion is, I must be getting old.

You define the situation as real; look for clues to confirm it, like forgetting something, and it becomes real in its consequence. You reinforce the connection between re-tirement and growing old.

"If we look the research on memory and age, in general, it supports the assumption that age has a negative effect on short-term memory. Interestingly, age seems to have a positive effect on long-term memory, but that is another issue. The main issue is that when researchers compare two different groups of people who differ by age, and when they find differences in memory scores, they assume that age caused these differences. I for one, question this assumption."

To carry this thought forward I asked, "Can anyone think of another explanation, other than age, that might explain why older people do not do as well on short-term memory tests?"

This caused a moment of silence and then Lynn said, "Is it because our brains have more information; we have more to remember?"

"I'm afraid not," I replied.

To give them a hint, I asked, "When somebody does research on memory and age, where do you think the young subjects in this research come from?"

"School, they're students," Lynn replied.

"Of course, and what are university students supposed to devote their time to? Studying, naturally, so we find that the young people who take part in this research are university students who spend most of their time exercising their short-term memory. Besides, students are used to writing exams and do not feel intimidated by researchers in lab coats. No wonder they do better on short-term memory tests.

"The older subjects, on the other hand, do not exercise their short-term memory as often or as intensely as the younger students, and many are not as comfortable in a research situation.

"It is quite possible that you are starting to forget things as you get older. However, the reason is not necessarily the aging process or mind deterioration. It is *because you do not exercise your short-term memory* as much as you used to.

"When you were younger and just starting out, you were learning new things every day. You were learning how to perform your job, meeting new people, remembering which child wants what sandwich in their lunch, remembering when to take the children to hockey practice, piano lessons, and so on. As time passes, when the job becomes second nature and the children leave home, your short-term memory can begin to coast.

"As with most bodily functions," I explained, "short-term memory is a function of use. The adage, 'use it or lose it' applies just as readily to short-term memory as to muscle strength. I have met people who returned to school after their children have grown. When asked if their short-term memory had improved, without exception they told me that it improved significantly. The reason it improved is because they were beginning to exercise their short-term memory."

Neurological research supports this conclusion. In a book entitled *The Brain that Changes Itself*, the author cites various research studies that confirm that the brain can rejuvenate itself through use and this includes improvements in memory loss.[2] If you expect to forget things as you grow older, it can become a self-fulfilling prophecy and you can hasten the mental decline of the use-it-or-lose-it brain.

In another study of nearly 3000 people aged 65 to 94, those given ten hours of training in memory, problem solving, and decision-making tasks over the course of several weeks showed marked and lasting increases in cognitive ability. 'Booster' training sessions received a year later resulted in further improvement in mental function, which persisted for over a year.[3]

For additional support of this conclusion, suggestions came forth that "The mature brain may lose some of the processing speed and accuracy that the younger brain has, but it isn't inferior. The mature brain organizes differently. Especially when it is adequately challenged, it keeps growing and developing new strengths and assets that the average younger brain cannot compete with because of the reservoirs of knowledge that we have - what we sometimes call wisdom." [4]

I can suggest a research project for anyone who is interested in this subject. Many older people have gone back to university. The research would involve a group of young students and a group of older students and testing their short-term memory. This way they would be comparing apples to apples and I feel confident that the older students would do as well as the younger students on a short-term memory test. The conclusion would be that it is not age that affects memory, but usage.

If you find that you are starting to forget things, you have several options. You can get involved in activities that will exercise your short-term memory, such as going back to school, joining a theater group where you have to memorize lines, or you can memorize the phone book. These exercises will definitely improve your short-term memory. Alternatively, and this is my preference, you can stop worrying or blaming your age and just accept what is happening - you are not exercising your short-term memory as much as you used to.

I am not denying that some elderly people experience memory loss due to physiological changes or problems. My point is that when short-term memory begins to fail you should not consider it as a sign that you are getting old or senile. People who worry about their memory convince themselves that there is something wrong and that it relates to growing old, or to being re-tired. Re-tirement can affect short-term memory only if your mind stagnates.

The self-fulfilling prophecy is not always working in a negative direction. "The beauty of the self-fulfilling prophecy," I said, "is that it can work for you, rather than against you. If you truly believe, and you should, that re-tirement is like winning a lottery, and that you will find worthwhile and enjoyable pursuits, you have a far better chance of succeeding. Don't get bogged down with the Ageist Self-fulfilling Prophecy, and don't look for signs to confirm that you are getting old. Instead, look for signs to confirm your advantageous situation. You will find them; they are everywhere."

Mid-Life Crisis Re-defined

I turned my attention to Lynn and asked, "If you don't mind my asking, how old are you Lynn?"

She smiled, hesitated, and said, "No, I don't mind. I'm 62."

"The reason I asked is I get the impression that your concerns are not solely directed toward re-tirement."

"Well, I guess that's true," she said. "The problem is my life feels sort of flat now. I have a good law practice and things are going well, but I don't know. Something is missing. That's why when Dave mentioned re-tirement it perked my interest. I realize now that just having money is not enough. I have to find alternatives to keep me busy. However, it's true, I probably won't re-tire for a few years yet."

"It sounds to me, Lynn; you may be experiencing a mid-life crisis."

"You may be right," she replied.

"In that case, I would be happy to share my views of this issue. They may give you a new way of making sense of this problem. And even though your re-tirement is a few years away, it might just turn out to be a cure for this malaise."

"OK," she replied.

There has been a great deal of research on the so-called mid-life crisis and volumes of books written on it. Through my workshop experience, I have developed a few insights that I wanted to share with Lynn and the others. Admittedly, my approach and analysis is somewhat simplistic, but I felt it could shed some light on an issue that can be misunderstood.

Therefore, in response to Lynn's concern I said, "One way to look at the middle-age crisis is to view it as the 'systematic elimination of unanswered questions and goals'. This may sound somewhat formal but to understand this, think back to when you were much younger. At that time, your future was infinite. You had everything to look forward to and your head was full of questions and expectations about what your future held. I am sure you wondered if, when, and who you would marry, how many children you would have, what they would be like, where you would live, what type of work you would pursue, how rich you would be, and so on. Your head was full of unanswered questions about what might lie ahead in your future. The last thing on your mind was re-tirement."

"Suddenly you have reached a point in your life where most of your unanswered questions have been answered - some to your satisfaction and others not to your satisfaction. You know if and whom you would marry, how rich you would be, and so on. The only major unanswered question that lies ahead is re-tirement, the last thing on your mind when you were younger. If you are not totally satisfied with some aspect of your life and you feel it is too late to make any changes, if your life no longer includes many unanswered questions or goals, and the thought of re-tiring scares you, do not lose heart. Re-tirement can be your saving grace.

"Let's take a more critical look at middle-age. What exactly does the term imply? To my mind, it suggests a mid-point in the progression from birth to death. This image portrays life as linear suggesting that it follows a straight line based on a single dimension - age. In addition, by focusing on a mid-point between birth and death, it implies that the second half will involve losses and that it will not be as good as the first half. Middle age is halfway to the end. No wonder it can be scary.

"The good news is this description is not totally accurate. Life experiences from the past and into the future are not linear nor based solely on age. People are not one-dimensional. Our incomes, levels of education, individual skills, confidence levels, family status, net worth, to name but a few, change over the life span and will continue to change into the future. At certain points, any one of these dimensions may be on the rise, on a level plane, or on the decline. We are the sum total of our experiences.

"I am not denying that life can be quite different when you re-tire. However, to reflect the process of transition more accurately, I suggest rather than identifying a mid-point between life and death, we focus on what I call the 'Centerpoint' of life.

Centerpoint

"The Centerpoint is when the individual re-tires with a dash, changes from a work to a re-tirement career, and gets a 'new set of wheels'. It involves drawing on past experiences to plan a new career that encompasses the best of their work and leisure careers. It doesn't matter how long you take to process the fusion of your work and leisure careers, the important point is the benefits gained through the process. If you have an exciting re-tirement to look forward to, or are experiencing a re-tirement that is worthwhile and enjoyable, you have re-introduced a series of goals and unanswered questions to your life. In so doing, you will either not experience, or at least minimize, the mid-life crisis."

My reference to the Centerpoint is not simply a marketing ploy (like a retirement home). It is a more accurate way to describe the convergence of your work and leisure careers. This new concept did not exist for past generations because they were less likely to be able to step back and plan for their life following their working career. Re-tirees today are lucky to have this opportunity. In addition, you do not have to be re-tired to begin this planning process. In fact, it is preferable that it begins well before re-tirement.

"I encourage you," I continued, "to look on this period of your life not as middle-age, but as a staging point and the ideal opportunity to prepare yourself for your re-tirement career. Use this opportunity to re-introduce unanswered questions and goals to your life. Your unanswered questions and goals for the future will probably be quite different from those that you eliminated up to this point. For the future, you may wonder how you can apply some of your knowledge and skills to benefit others, how you can satisfy your needs and skills through different activities, how your re-tirement career will unfold, and so on. If you re-introduce questions and goals to your life, you will replace your malaise with optimism."

I had spoken at length about an issue that I felt was very important. To see if my arguments hit home, I asked Dave, "Well, have I convinced you that re-tirement has nothing to do with growing old?"

"You have," said Dave. "I can see that when I re-tire it doesn't mean that I am old. I really didn't stop to think of it that way."

"Hearing what you have to say," said Diane, "especially the part about the self-fulfilling prophecy, makes me feel younger."

"That's great," I replied.

"By the way, does anyone know how and why age rather than say performance is used to determine when a person can or has to re-tire?"

"I think I read somewhere that it started in Germany," said Lynn.

"That's right. Prince Otto Von Bismarck set up the world's first pension plan in Germany in 1889 and benefits began at age 70. There are several interesting side notes to this piece of history. Firstly, most people at that time did not live beyond age 70. Secondly, it established an arbitrary age as the basis for re-tirement; and when a person could draw a pension. This has remained until today. Interestingly, Bismarck lived to be 83 and continued to work well beyond his 70th birthday."

"It's possible that I will still be at work when I am 70," said Dave.

"There's nothing wrong with that," I replied. "As long as you are enjoying it. My main point is that just because we use age to initiate a pension, do not assume that re-tirement relates to aging or getting old. That may have been the case in the past, but conditions today are completely different from the past."

From Hippies, to Yuppies, to.....?

"In fact if you think about it, you should consider yourselves lucky to be re-tiring now rather than in the past."

"What do you mean?" asked Lynn.

"Look at your situation. Why do you think people who re-tire now or who will soon re-tire, are better off compared to retirees in the past?"

"I suppose they'll have more money," Dave answered.

"For sure," I said. "On the average, you are richer than any generation of retirees before you. While you were developing your career, private and public pension plans enabled you to establish an adequate financial base for re-tirement, and you were aware of the need to save and invest for re-tirement. That's why you found a financial planner."

"Anything else?" I asked.

"We are healthier and people today will live longer," Craig replied.

"Absolutely, science and medicine have progressed to control or eliminate many diseases, and it has become part of our culture to watch what we eat and to exercise."

I added, "The Boomers are also lucky because they are more educated and have a greater sense of personal fulfillment with greater expectations for fulfillment in re-tirement compared to past generations of retirees. Finally, there are more Boomers than any generation of retirees in the past. This gives them political and economic clout."

"So," I re-emphasized, "you are lucky to be re-tiring now rather than in the past."

"I guess so," said Dave. "But I don't think it was all luck. We worked hard to be able to re-tire."

"I don't mean lucky in that sense," I said. "Don't forget, I defined the new re-tirement as an earned career. And implicit in the word '*earned*' is the fact that you did not rely entirely on luck."

I directed my comment to Dave and said, "Do you remember the old image of retirement (without the dash) that we talked about earlier - retirement as withdrawal from work? Well there was some truth in that image in the past. But because of various conditions that did not exist a generation or two ago, I think that you are lucky to be re-tiring now rather than in the past."

"I guess so," said Lynn.

"If you think about it," I said, "we don't have a name or word to describe the Boomers when they re-tire. When the Boomers were younger, they were called Hippies, and then they became Yuppies. So the question is, what shall we call them when they re-tire?"

To respond to this question first we have to define two concepts that are often confused - a cohort and a generation. A cohort refers to everyone born during a certain period of time. The Boomers are a cohort that includes everyone born between 1946 and 1964. A generation includes everyone who shares common cultural or social characteristics and attitudes. Hippies are an example of a generation.

The term Hippies referred to a way of thinking and a set of values relating to their lifestyle of political activism, cannabis, peace, the new age, music and art. Of course, not all young people at that time displayed the so-called Hippie lifestyle, but the term applied to the entire Boomer cohort in the past.

When the Boomers entered the workforce, their behavior and attitudes changed. Most pursued careers and spent money with a vengeance and the term Yuppie emerged. This stood for Young Urban Professionals and it related to their education, work, and living status. Again, not all working Boomers were urban professionals, but the label became common.

"When the Boomers re-tire," I continued, "the term Yuppies will be obsolete. They are no longer young, many will not live in urban areas, and when they re-tire, they will no longer be at work. We need a new term to describe all re-tired Boomers, regardless of their educational, economic, and attitudinal differences."

"We can call them re-tired Boomers," said Diane.

"That's one way to look at it," I replied. "But do you remember why I said you were lucky to be re-tiring now?"

"Sort of," Dave said. "We are richer and will live longer. There were other reasons but I can't remember all of them."

"Well, I suggest we refer to re-tiring Boomers as Luckies.

"I guess you are right," said Lynn. "When I look at my parents or grandparents' generation, things are definitely better now."

"Additionally, who knows what the future holds," I added. "Things may not be as good for future generations of re-tirees. So you are definitely lucky to be re-tiring now."

"But another important advantage," I continued, "is that society's image of re-tirement is changing for the better, and this in turn will influence your self-image as a re-tiree. Re-tirement is becoming something to be proud of and this is based mainly on economic considerations."

I explained that each segment of society develops and retains a sense of self-importance, or lack of importance, in part, due to its economic buying power. Clearly, pre-Boomer retirees were not significant in terms of numbers, they did not live very long after retirement, and they did not have economic clout. They simply did not represent a market large enough to be pursued by the providers of goods and services. Advertising aimed at older people in the past generally focused on health aids and other non re-tirement entities. TV in the past rarely included retired people and if they did, it was negatively. It was as though they did not exist.

"But things will be different when you re-tire," I said. "You represent a huge identifiable market the suppliers of clothing, entertainment, cosmetics, food, cars, motorcycles, travel, to name but a few, will continue to court you, especially in re-tirement. When the Boomers were younger, to attract their attention, advertising agencies portrayed happy, lively, healthy, sexy, young people enjoying whatever it was they had to sell. This enabled the Boomers to develop a strong positive image of being the most advantageous group in society. Do you remember the phrase 'never trust anyone over 30'? This arrogance reflected a sense of self-importance spawned by the economic power of the Boomers when they were young. It was easy to feel proud of being a Hippie and a Yuppie because they held economic and political power.

"The beauty of re-tiring now is the Boomers will retain their political and economic clout into re-tirement and the suppliers of goods and services will continue to court them with vigor. As a result, they will portray re-tirees differently from the past. They will be seen as happy, lively, healthy, sexy, older people enjoying whatever advertisers wish to sell to this economically powerful cohort."

I told them to think of the significance of this major shift; and how it will affect society's image of re-tirement. When the Boomers re-tire, they will consist of millions of people with nothing but time and money on their hands and they are just itching to find happiness that eluded many of them while they were at work. I am willing to bet the barn that the image of re-tirement is in for a dramatic change.

"The signs are everywhere," I said. "For example, why do you think the major clothing manufacturers introduced loose fitting or relaxed jeans a few years ago? Do you think this is simply a fashion statement? When I was a kid, loose fitting jeans were called 'huskies'. If you had to buy huskies, it meant you couldn't fit into regular fitting jeans. Today, clothing manufacturers want to continue selling to us but many of us need huskies and the word huskies is not flattering. To overcome this conundrum, the manufacturers simply repackaged huskies as relaxed fitting. The product is the same; only the name and its image have changed."

"I know of another example," said Lynn. "Up until a few years ago, every winter my son and I drove to Florida. We stopped at a particular fast food restaurant as part of our routine. A few years ago, we stopped at the restaurant and the area they had split in half the area called Play Land. Now they had the play area for the kids on one side and a player piano on the other side."

"That's a good example," I said. "Clearly the fast food industry has realized the importance of older Boomers as customers and has begun to accommodate their interests. This is the tip of the iceberg. We see the popularity of music from the 60's and 70's. If you flip through the radio dial, it seems as though there are as many stations playing the hits from the past as those playing today's music. Additionally, if you check the newsstand you will find many new magazines that cater to re-tirees. This was unheard of in the past."

"That makes a lot of sense," said Lynn. "But it may be easier said than done."

Dave said to Lynn, "Diane and I went through the Life Goal Planning program with our friends a few weeks ago. It has definitely given me some guidance and I am beginning to see more clearly what I can do when I re-tire."

"It's never too early to begin thinking about how you will spend your time and how to satisfy your needs and skills in re-tirement," I said.

At that point, Dave's grandson came over and pulled him away from the discussion. As the party was beginning to break up, I excused myself and withdrew to find my wife. As I left, I said, "Don't forget now, keep buying those relaxed jeans."

Chapter Summary

- Re-tirement is not an aging issue.
- To re-tire is to change from a work to a re-tirement career and if you believe that when you re-tire you are getting old or that others will think of you that way, you are guilty of the Ageist Self-fulfilling Prophecy. That is, you may look for signs to prove or validate your belief and if you look hard enough, you will find them even if you have to create them.

8

WITH A LITTLE HELP FROM MY FRIENDS

(The Beatles, 1967)

SPOUSAL RELATIONSHIPS, SINGLE IN RE-TIREMENT, AND FRIENDSHIPS

The phone rang in my office and it was Janice. "I don't know if you remember me," she said, "I am Les's wife. We met at Dave and Diane's house about a month ago."

"Of course I remember, Janice. What can I do for you?" I asked.

She confessed that she was having a problem with Les. She sounded worried and I asked her to explain the problem.

"I didn't want to talk about this when we met at Diane's house," she said, "but there are two problems. Les has changed completely since he retired a year ago. I don't know what to do. He is talking about moving and I'm not sure I want to go."

"How has he changed, Janice?" I asked.

"He is making my life miserable by hanging over my neck 24 hours a day. He criticizes my cooking, he has to go grocery shopping with me and decide on everything I put in the cart. When the phone rings, he runs to answer, although no one ever calls him, and he stands around while I talk. When the conversation is over, he wants to know all the details. He never cared before. Last summer we had a lovely lawn with flowerbeds. He dug up everything and planted a vegetable garden. We had vegetables coming out of our ears. Then he got mad because I wouldn't preserve it all. The last straw was this week when the car insurance came due. He never said a word to me - just sold my car. Please tell me what to do. I'm at my wits end." *

She explained that she saw a letter in an advice column in the newspaper and the description sounded exactly like Les.

"The thing that really worries me," Janice said sounding quite upset, "is the advice they gave is that the husband should see a neurologist (brain surgeon). And if that didn't work, the wife should seek counseling. What should I do?"

After listening to Janice's problem, I suggested we take this one-step at a time.

"Although your problem sounds extreme," I said, "it is important to look first at the advice you found in the newspaper, then we can take a look at how to overcome this problem."

She agreed.

"First of all," I explained, "the advice in the paper is misguided and based on a false image of retirement. It's a good example of what I referred to as retirement without the dash and of certain writers, in this case a journalist, making false assumptions on the relationship between retirement and health. The suggestion that Les or the husband in the article should see a neurologist assumes that retirement is a disease."

I reminded her that re-tirement does not cause brain or nerve damage and it would be a complete waste of everyone's time for Les to see a neurologist. I am willing to bet that his nervous system is intact. The next piece of advice, that the wife seeks counseling, is also a waste of time. Why? The problem lies with the husband's behavior and nothing will be gained if the wife sees a counselor.

With that out of the way, I said, "Forget about the article. What do you think is the problem?"

"I don't know," she replied. "But it has become my problem too."

"If you think back to what we talked about at Diane's house," I said, "it seems to me that the problem is really quite obvious. Les is looking desperately for something to do; he's bored. In addition, to make matters worse, he is interfering with your life and activities. In other words, he is trying to replace satisfactions lost from work through his home and your activities. He tried being a cook, shopper, telephone operator, and a gardener. But these activities were fleeting - busy work - and have not brought him happiness."

"I couldn't agree with you more," said Janice. "But what can we do?"

I had a few suggestions that I felt could help her situation, but it would be best if we included Les in the discussion. I suggested that they both meet at my office the following week.

I suggested that she not tell Les about the newspaper advice column because frankly, it was way off the mark. She should simply tell him that we could get together again to see how his re-tirement was progressing. We could talk about this issue and his thoughts about moving. Janice was delighted with my suggestion.

The following week when she and Les came to my office, to begin the conversation I asked Les how re-tirement was progressing. He told me that he was starting to apply some of the exercises we went through and that he was thinking about moving. I took this as my cue and asked where he was planning to move.

"Janice and I love the outdoors, so we were thinking about moving west to be near the mountains."

"You mean you were thinking about moving," Janice said to Les. "I'm really not so sure. I told Les the other day, I'm not sure that I would be happy leaving here. We have our friends and our daughter and her family live here."

"But if we move," Les responded, "we can be closer to Richard and his family. Actually, there are a few things Janice and I are trying to come to grips with since I re-tired. Moving is just one of them."

"The biggest problem," Janice said to me, "is Les is always underfoot. I keep telling him to find something else to do, but it doesn't seem to work."

Les responded, "I admit that I have been spending a fair amount of time at home. But some of my best friends are still working."

"This can present problems," I said. "And there is no question that re-tirement can affect the marriage relationship. So if you would like, I will go over some of the points that are worth thinking about on this issue."

"I think that would be a good idea," said Janice.

"So do I," said Les. "But, is this a common problem?"

"I wouldn't say it's common," I replied. "But re-tirement can change the ground rules in a marriage and it is very important that you spend a little time thinking about the amount and quality of time you spend together."

I explained that when a family is young, most of the leisure time spent together is with the children. As time moves on, with the children growing up and leaving home, and with the husband and or wife re-tiring, the daily rhythm of time together and apart is likely to change. With the freeing up of time no longer occupied by work, an adjustment in the amount of time a couple spends together may be necessary.

Communication

"One of the most important things you both have to look at," I explained, "is communication, and true communication is crucial when it comes to planning for re-tirement."

Obviously, I had no idea of the inner workings of their marriage, so I spoke about this in general terms and shared with them an example from a workshop. In this case, we were discussing housing and I asked for a show of hands from those people who were thinking about moving after re-tirement. Several people raised their hand including one man whose wife turned to him and said with a somewhat surprised look on her face, 'I didn't know we were thinking of moving!'

They both smiled at this point and I said, "It is fairly safe to assume that they were not communicating about re-tirement."

"But Janice and I have talked about moving," said Les.

"Yes, I realize that." I replied. "I gave this as an example of a couple who were not communicating their re-tirement plans. My main point is, regardless of the level of communication between a couple, re-tirement is a necessary topic of discussion because it is a shared experience and the more you know of each other's feelings, the more likely is the transition to go smoothly. So sit down together and clarify your feelings. Talk about how you plan to spend your time. What you plan to do apart and what you plan to do together. You may not have an immediate answer to these questions, but it is important to start thinking and talking in this direction."

I turned to Janice and asked, "When you talked to Les about this problem, were you criticizing him or discussing a solution to the problem?"

"I don't know the solution," she replied. "So I guess I have been criticizing him. We tried to talk after the session with you but we didn't get very far."

"That's OK," I said. "It's a start and Les may have felt frustrated by his situation and it is affecting his ability to talk about it. I have a suggestion that may help, but first let's take a look at the second issue; Janice's concern that you are interfering with her domain."

"That's a good way to put it," said Janice.

Respect Each Other's Territory

I turned to Les and said, "Let me ask you a question, Les. Suppose you were still working. How do you think you would feel if Janice came to work with you and the first day on the job began to criticize and tell you how to do things better?"

Les smiled but did not answer my question. When I ask this question in my workshop as you can imagine, this hits the nail right on the head and a lively discussion usually follows.

To emphasize my point further, I told them the story of Howard. He was happily re-tired, involved in civic duties, and loved to spend time in his basement workshop. One day when his wife was out, he decided to rearrange the kitchen to make it more efficient.

When his wife came home, she never said a word. Howard assumed that she was pleased with his interior design capabilities. Later, when he was out for the day, his wife went into his workshop and rearranged his tools the way she thought they should be.

"With this example," I said, "although Howard's wife did not say anything, she was communicating. Her message was - don't touch my stuff. I met another woman whose husband had taken over the household duties when he re-tired, and she was concerned that he would not give them back to her when she re-tired.

"Les, I am not suggesting that you should steer clear of Janice's domain. I know some husbands who get involved in the kitchen or housework and the wife is delighted. My only suggestion is that you discuss this issue with Janice. Sit down and rationally examine the extent to which Janice would feel comfortable having you get involved in her domain. Let's face it Les, I would imagine that Janice has done a great job up until now. Just because you are re-tired it doesn't necessarily mean that you can interfere.

"As you both know," I said, "to come up with a solution you have to understand the problem."

"The problem is," said Janice, "Les is interfering with my life."

I turned to Les and asked, "Would you agree that this is an accurate assessment of the problem?"

"I suppose so," he responded.

"Then the solution is for you to find interests that are not simply 'busywork'. As we discussed a few weeks ago, you have to find activities that will enable you to replace satisfactions lost from work. Moreover, I might add, that do not interfere with Janice's life. Would you say that would be the solution to the problem?" I asked.

"Most definitely," said Janice.

"What do you think, Les?" I asked.

"I guess so," he replied. "For instance, one thing I have enjoyed for years is playing bridge. I would love it if Janice joined me. She tried it but she really didn't like it. That might solve part of the problem. But I can't seem to convince her to try."

I replied with a question. "Les, what do you think the chances are of Janice enjoying bridge after you re-tired if she didn't like it before? What does your re-tirement have to do with it?"

"I don't know," said Les. "I was just hoping she would like it."

"Am I correct in assuming that you are a pretty good bridge player and Janice would be a beginner?" I asked. "That may be part of the reason she didn't like it."

"Well that's true," replied Les. "But I encouraged her to take lessons and she didn't want to."

"Well, I think you have your answer. You have to face the fact that Janice does not share your love of bridge, and that your re-tiring will not change her feelings on this issue."

"I guess you are right. There's nothing I can do," Les lamented.

"Actually there is something you can do," I said. "If you think about it Les, you just mentioned two needs that you would like to satisfy when you re-tire. One is to continue playing bridge, and the other is to have Janice join you. You have spent many years playing bridge without her and this may have to continue. However, your desire and need to share a re-tirement activity with Janice can flourish. The only thing is, you will probably have to satisfy this need through a different activity. Re-tirement gives both of you the freedom to develop a new activity together, something that you are both starting at the ground floor. This way you can satisfy your need for doing something together, even though it is not through bridge.

"If you want to start something new together, you can approach this the same way I showed you the other day at Dave and Diane's house. In this case, you each should take a look at the other person's Needs and Skills List and develop a combined list that includes needs and skills that apply to both of you. Then brainstorm an activity that you can both take part in."

I explained further, "I don't want you to get the wrong impression. It's true that you two have a few things to work out, but eventually you will find that the freedom of re-tirement will enhance your relationship. Nevertheless, the bottom line Les is you have to start applying the tools we went through at Dave's house. You can't rely on Janice to pick up where work left off. It's not fair, and in all likelihood, it's not possible."

Single in Re-tirement

Obviously not everyone is in a couple situation before or after they re-tire. Approximately 44% of seniors are single (widowed, never married, separated or divorced) and this is based on midlife divorce, outliving a spouse, or choosing not to marry. Because women tend to live longer and marry younger than men, they are more likely to be single in re-tirement. On the other hand, many men and women may choose to be single before or after they re-tire. But let's start by looking online. If you Google this topic most of the results focus on the financial side, especially to start planning early, and educate yourself. Definitely sound advice. On the non-financial side, in addition to dating sites for single re-tirees, one finds topics such as:

- Staying healthy
- Dealing with divorce
- Looking for work
- Looking for love
- Social & emotional well being
- Housing needs
- Travel

My point is, yes these can be important, but most apply to life in general rather then re-tirement. Being single by choice or not, and whether this situation is desirable or not, extends much beyond the scope of re-tirement. Nevertheless, to see how Life Goal Planning can add a fresh approach to this situation, when you complete the Life

Goal Planning Workshop (Part 3 of the workbook), check out the Single in Re-tirement exercise at end of the workshop instructions.

Friendships

I wanted to mention a statement Les made earlier so I said, "Les, if I recall correctly, did you indicate that one of your problems is that some of your friends are still at work?"

"Yes," he replied. "I have to admit it. I miss going to work and seeing my friends."

"That's perfectly understandable," I said. "Let's face it. You have spent a long time at work and probably made quite a few good friends. These are people you saw almost everyday, and you share many common experiences. They can sympathize with you when something goes wrong at work, and can truly appreciate when something goes right. On the other hand, there may be people at work who you are happy never to see again. In any case, your work experience is the basis of a common bond, and when this is missing, as can happen with re-tirement, it can affect friendships."

"The question that many people must face," I explained, "is what might become of their friendship when they re-tire? For example, because you are out of the picture you will not be aware of many changes in the workplace and this may affect the nature of your friendship. You may know of someone who re-tired and continues to show up at work just to keep up with what is happening there."

"I'm one of them," admitted Les. "At least I used to do that but I don't do that any more. But like you said, some of my friends, like Dave, are still at work and I don't get to see them as much as I used to."

"It is also possible," I said, "that if you and a friend from work re-tired at the same time, your re-tirement careers may develop in different directions."

"I suppose that's true," said Les.

Giving up contact with colleagues and patients can be particularly problematic. It was the most frequently mentioned drawback to re-tirement, and as we saw earlier, mixing with people was a key reason for working in re-tirement, and the most frequently mentioned loss from work. Here are a few examples.

Missing seeing our simply wonderful patients, many of whom, became dear friends!

Miss interaction with my patients who were my friends, but they wish me well in this new phase of life. We live in a great little town, have met many wonderful people, and have yet to be bored. We have retained friends from pre-retirement days, and still see them

Main drawback is related to change of geography regarding living. I am too far away from friends to see them on a casual basis. I have to plan a trip of an entire day to see them for social activities. While I am at work or work related activities there are plenty of social resources. It is only after work or on the weekends when it is difficult.

Missing the personal contact with the patients that you have had through a 36 year career. The feeling in retirement of not being a productive member of society.

Not seeing my great staff and partners as much. Not interacting with patients as much.

"The main point," I continued, "is that now may be a good time to solidify your present friendships and to expand your friendship circle. For some people this will not present a problem. However, for others, this is easier said than done. So, why not set out on some sort of campaign? Extend yourself a little. Be willing to take some risks. Seek people out. Talk to them. Start a conversation with someone at a meeting or ball game. In fact, this ties in nicely with Les's search to find re-tirement activities. Join a club, take a course at a community college, volunteer for something, or join a health club. Do whatever it takes to get in touch with new people, your source for companionship, support, approval, security, encouragement, and affection. You never know what will come out of this until you try."

Interrupted when my telephone rang, I excused myself to take the call.

Chapter Summary

- Key issues to look at include communication, respecting each other's territory, and creating activities together.
- Communication is critical in the decision for both spouses to re-tire at the same time.
- Giving up contact with colleagues can be particularly problematic. It was the most frequently mentioned drawback to re-tirement, a key reason for working in re-tirement, and the most frequently mentioned loss from work.

9

OUR HOUSE

(Graham Nash, 1970)

MOVING IN RE-TIREMENT

After I got off the phone was time to look at Janice's other concern, moving. This is a common issue in re-tirement and the problem is, the more traditional approach seems to miss the most important elements of this issue. For instance, it is common to focus on the pros and cons of various types of housing (e.g. condominiums, apartments, co-ops, mobile homes, retirement communities, and so on). I call this the real estate approach. This issue may be important, but it ignores the more critical issues, like the one faced by Janice and Les, in the context of changing from a work to a re-tirement career. Their concern goes beyond the real estate issue.

Within the context of the traditional approach, housing issues are often subject to generalities. For example, a couple who participated in my workshop told me about a course they attended where the speaker referred to a stress level chart which stated that retirement was a high stress situation. As such, the speaker warned that one should not consider moving until at least one year following retirement.

To re-quote an expression I used earlier - hogwash. To me this is a classic 'retire without the dash' blanket statement. There are three things wrong with this statement. First, it is a sweeping generalization, which in itself has no place in re-tirement planning. Second, re-tirement is not necessarily a high stress situation. In many cases, re-tirement can lower stress. Third, moving at re-tirement can sometimes be a wise decision.

Not everyone wants to move at re-tirement. Many people prefer to stay where they are and have no desire to move at all. Having said that, re-tirement can trigger a housing move. In fact, it can be the perfect time to change your housing situation. Many people at our workshop actively consider moving after they re-tire. Some think about moving to a small town or the cottage; others think about moving back to their place of birth. Many plan to spend the winter months in a warmer climate, while others plan to move to a different - usually smaller - home or condominium within the same city or community. I even met a couple at a workshop who built a bigger home in re-tirement. Everyone has different needs and priorities and it is clear that the decision to move goes well beyond financial or real estate considerations. Moving after re-tirement requires careful consideration, especially if, as in Janice's case, one person wants to move and the other does not.

Rather than tell Les and Janice what they should do, I wanted to make them aware of a few housing considerations that contribute to re-tirement happiness. I turned to Les and said, "You mentioned that you would like to move but it seems that this may present problems for Janice. Why do you want to move?"

"I think we would be better off if we move," said Les.

"Better off in what way?" I asked.

"Well, we can save money by moving to a smaller community and we both love the outdoors. We usually spend our summers camping and fishing and we both love to ski. I don't have a spot picked out yet. Nevertheless, I thought that if we moved to a small city near the mountains, we would have the best of both worlds. Besides, if we sold our house we would have more money to live off."

"Your reasoning sounds good," I said. "But the problem is, it doesn't seem to be in sync with Janice's plans. So let's take a look at Janice's concern and see if you can find a solution, or at least a compromise."

I asked them if they knew anyone who moved after re-tirement and who, after moving, realized it was a mistake.

"Well, yes," said Les. "This guy I used to work with and his wife moved back to England. They stayed about six months and didn't like it. I heard that they moved back."

"Like all issues in re-tirement," I said, "just because you know of one case where a plan did not work out, it does not necessarily follow that it will not work out for you. Having said that, we can learn a few things from your friend's experience, and certainly the decision to move should not be treated lightly."

I advised them to think about two very important questions. Firstly, can you satisfy your needs and skills in the new community? Next, if it doesn't work out, what are your alternatives? You don't want to feel trapped there.

"Sometimes it's impossible to predict what it will be like living in a new community," I said, "until after the move. You have to expect the unexpected. You may miss old friends, the doctor who looked after you for years, your mechanic who you trust, your standing in the community, and familiar places filled with memories. And then again, re-tirement is a great opportunity for a new beginning."

My main concern was that they thought this through thoroughly, and reached a mutually agreed upon compromise. To start their thinking I told them about Sylvia who moved and encountered an unexpected problem. Here's what happened.

Sylvia was a widow. After she re-tired, she moved back to a small town where she came from to be near her family. She always enjoyed holidays back home, so now that she was free to live where she wanted, moving home seemed like a good idea. At first things went well but after a while she began to feel stifled by her family. They were always thinking about her and were concerned that she not be lonely. Therefore, whenever her family members entertained they always included Sylvia. In return, when she entertained she felt obliged to invite her family.

However, Sylvia wasn't lonely. She wanted to develop new friendships outside of her family sphere but constantly being with family kept her from developing new friendships. Because she was living in a small town, she wasn't meeting anyone new. Her friendships were limited. She longed for the sense of independence she used to feel. Unfortunately, she had sold her original home, housing prices began to rise, and she couldn't afford to buy another house in her former community. She eventually moved back to the city she used to live in, rented an apartment, and continues to visit her family for special occasions only - as she used to do before she re-tired.

After I finished relating this story to Les and Janice, they looked a little pensive.

"I'm not trying to talk you out of moving," I said. "I'm just warning you to be cautious when moving because you never know what it will be like until you move there."

Among your re-tirement mentors, 23% moved after they re-tired. Of these, 79% moved far enough away that they had to establish new friends. Re-tirement can be the perfect time to change your housing situation.

Moving after re-tirement requires careful consideration. Having said that, the current housing market may have added a new wrinkle to the decision to re-tire as some people may be relying on selling their home to help finance their re-tirement. Let's start by looking at why your re-tirement mentors decided to move.

Table 9-1. Reasons for Moving After Re-tirement

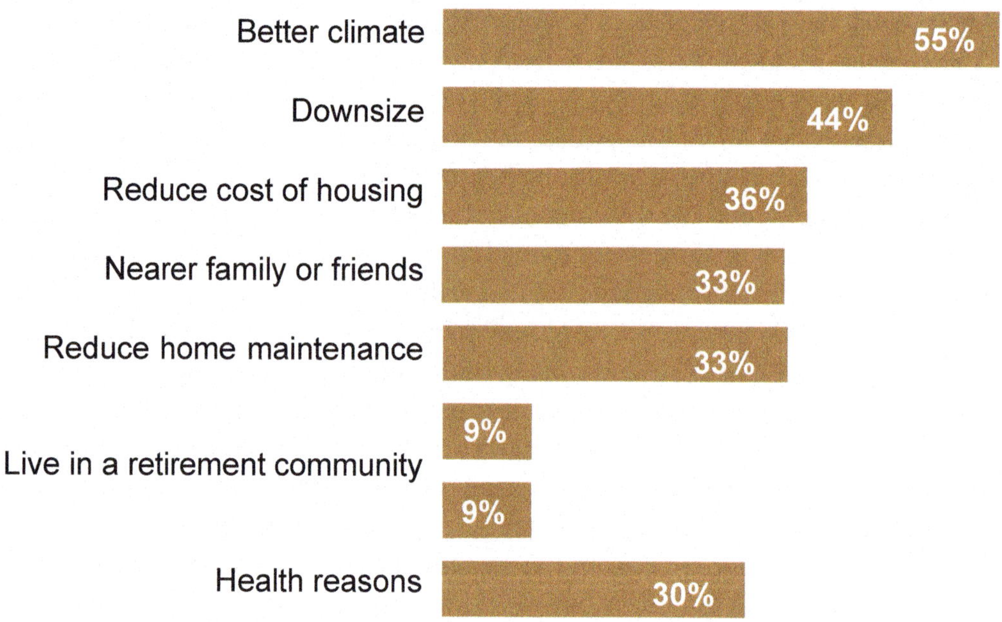

Other reasons for moving included:

To live on a lake, own a boat, be near kids and grand kids.

Snow skiing and living in the mountains.

Build house of dreams where I always wanted to live.

I moved back home.

I needed the physical change to allow myself the new freedom.

Lots of outdoor activities where we moved.

For change of lifestyle – we currently live on an island in (the Caribbean).

Could no longer afford two mortgages.

To a college town, more activities then small town I practiced in.

Don't Be Impulsive

To give them some guidelines, I said, "We can learn a few things from Sylvia's story. If you decide to move, the best piece of advice I can give you is don't be too impulsive and don't burn your bridges. Don't buy a home before knowing that it is right for you. This can lead to grief."

I told them about Greg and Sara's experience. They lived in the Mid-West and took a holiday to visit their children who lived on the coast. After spending a week with the kids, they took a side trip to a small town a few hours away. They came across a small house overlooking the ocean and Greg fell in love with it. According to Sara, Greg was all set to buy. This would be the re-tirement home of his dreams. She wasn't so sure, so she suggested that they wait until they had a chance to survey the area properly. They went back to spend a few more days with their children. Then they returned to that small town and after spending a few days there, realized this location was not right for them and had they bought it impulsively, it would have been a big mistake. Fortunately, Sara had the foresight to hold back on Greg's impulse.

"Buying impulsively can be disastrous," I said. "You never know what it will be like - or what you might miss - until you spend some time there."

I told them about a couple I met who moved from a big city to a small community. After a while, they began to miss their former neighbors. Although they used to live in a large city, they were part of a very tight community where they had very close ties. When they realized their mistake, they went back to their original neighborhood hoping to find a house to buy. They went door-to-door asking if anyone wanted to sell. Unfortunately, no one was willing. Eventually they bought a house four blocks away, but it was not the same. Being somewhat removed, they were not able to regain the tight friendships they gave up.

Satisfy Your Needs in the New Community

"Another important rule," I stressed, "is to ask yourself if you can satisfy your needs and skills in the new community. Can you find activities that are worthwhile and enjoyable? Of course, you may never know until you move. But this important condition should be kept in mind."

"As I mentioned, we like to do things outdoors so I don't think this will be a problem for us," said Les.

"You never know," I replied. "Let me tell you about somebody who encountered this problem after moving. His name is Stan and before he re-tired, he and his wife used to spend the winters in a resort town in California. They thought that this would be the perfect place to re-tire. The weather was good, they both enjoyed playing golf, and over the years, they had developed a small group of friends. So, when Stan re-tired they sold their house and purchased a small house in this community. They spent some time fixing it up and about a year later, they sold the house and bought a condominium. Six months later, they sold the condominium and bought another house.

"It became clear that their series of moves had nothing to do with housing per se. Stan was bored and kept busy by moving and fixing up the houses he bought. Sure he enjoyed golfing, and various other activities, but they didn't totally replace being at work. To compensate for this, he worked at moving. He didn't do this to make money; he was simply looking for something else to keep him busy. Eventually they moved back to their original home city, Stan became involved in a small business, and they have not moved since. They still visit California and thoroughly enjoy life."

Don't Burn Your Bridges

"Do you own your home?" I asked.

"Yes we do," said Janice.

"Then the next piece of advice I can offer is if you move, 'don't burn your bridges'. Don't sell everything without giving your newly adopted home a trial run. If possible, rent out your present home and rent accommodations in the region where you plan to move. This may not compare to owning a home in the new community, but think of this as insurance. After your trial period, you will then be able to judge what is best for you. If it doesn't work out, you still have your original house to move back to. If it works out, then make the move permanent by selling your house. Who knows, your house may be worth more after you rent it out for six months or a year. And by renting initially in the new community, you have flexibility after you learn more about where you want to live."

"Another piece of advice," I continued, "which may not apply to you, is don't succumb to pressures from well meaning friends or even your children. You be the judge. Think about the lifestyle you want and the kind of people you are."

I told them about a couple I met who lived in a large house that was becoming a burden to both of them. They were spending too much time cleaning, and repairing things around the house. They had dreams of moving to a small farm. Unfortunately, their son did not want them to sell the house. He still lived at home and if his parents sold the house, he would have nowhere to live. To avoid having to find and I suppose pay for his own place, he made his parents feel guilty for wanting to sell the family house.

"That really doesn't apply to us," said Les.

"I realize that," I replied, "I am telling you about a few situations I have come across because, as I mentioned before, you will never know what problems might come up after you move."

If the Decision is not Mutual

"OK," I said. "Let's take a look at the other slightly more thorny issue where Les wants to move but Janice doesn't."

I told them about Ann who said that her husband was an avid fisherman and hunter. When he re-tired, he wanted to move to a 40-acre property that was at least a 30-minute drive to civilization. Ann told us that she went with her husband to look at the property and she just sat in the car crying. She knew that if they moved there she would be bored out of her mind and would hate every minute of it. Clearly, she had a dilemma.

It is common for one person to want to move back to where he or she came from and the other wants to stay where they are. For example, I met a woman in my workshop who mentioned that her husband wanted to move back to Bermuda, his birthplace. However, she didn't want to move because she couldn't stand her in-laws. Sometimes those people who think about moving back home forget why they left in the first place. Situations where one person wants to move and the other doesn't may not have an easy solution. To minimize the potential problem, I emphasized to Les and Janice the need for compromise.

"Janice, if you decide to try a move and you haven't burned your bridges, do it with an open mind. If you expect to hate the new location, chances are it will become a self-fulfilling prophecy. It will come true. This means that both of you should work towards finding worthwhile and enjoyable pursuits in the new community. If you are both able to satisfy your needs and skills in the new community, then in all probability the move will turn into a positive experience. If not, and if you are not trapped, you can always move back to where you came from, or to another location."

People who think about moving after re-tirement may never get this thought out of their system until they try it. So, by all means, go for it. Having said that, you must be prepared to expect the unexpected, and not put yourself in a position where you are not able to either come back to where you came from, or move on to somewhere else. If it doesn't work out and if you are able to rectify the situation, you will have gained from the experience. You will have learned that your original thought of moving was not for you.

"Well," I asked, "has that helped your situation?"

"Yes it has," said Les. "I still really want to move and I know that it might be a problem for Janice. Nevertheless, and I think you will agree with me on this Janice, we both have some things to think about. The most important thing I have learned is that we shouldn't sell our house until we are sure about this move."

"And what are your thoughts on this, Janice?" I asked.

"I was thinking the same thing as Les. I guess I would be more willing to try it knowing that we had something to come back to."

I encouraged Les and Janice to continue talking and thinking about what we had discussed. I assured them again that many couples have faced similar problems and that they were not insurmountable. They thanked me and left feeling, I believe, optimistic about the future.

Here is some advice from your re-tirement mentors who moved after re-tirement.

Research Before You Move

Explore many sites, especially if you hadn't traveled much during your work years.

Know where you are going and what you are doing.

Know your objectives prior to the move.

Prepare prior to retiring. Check all different areas you are considering prior to retiring.

Research carefully and realize that what you enjoy on vacation, may not fit you full time.

Spend a lot of time looking at every community because they all have pluses but other factors you may find not to your liking. We made a list of things we wanted: 2 car garage, master on first floor, walk out basement, new construction, hardwood floors, etc. and found a development that had everything.

Test the waters before making a commitment to move away from social connections.

Test the waters first by 'renting' (at least 6 months)in your desired area before committing to buying property.

Practical Considerations

Be sure you are going to be in a location where there is public transportation to a major city. Also, nice to be 10 minutes from a regional medical center. Being in an elevator building is critical for future thinking.

Best to downsize.

Both you and spouse need to agree completely.

Make sure you plan thoroughly with your spouse including timelines.

Don't go too far away from children.

forget about your dream home - buy something affordable - with a master bedroom suite on the first floor and something your spouse will be able to maintain when you become disabled or die.

Move to where you vacation and be on vacation all the time.

Pick a warm climate without much or no snow. It's easier to shovel rain!

Relax for a few months. Think about what you want to do.

Rent, don't buy right away.

Think through what you will do with your days, try out some new activities.

Try the new location for a few seasons .

Meet New Friends

Be outgoing to obtain new friends.

Get involved with church, service organization, etc to meet new friends.

Get involved with volunteering, both in general and with dentistry!

Make sure that you are going to be busy enough to feel fulfilled in life. Although I am quite extroverted is has been difficult to establish a group of individuals for social activities which are non-work related.

Realize that it will take a good long while to re-establish friendships so expect to be lonely for awhile.

Stay busy, organizations bring new friends.

you must be outgoing and willing to make new friends.

Chapter Summary

- Do not be impulsive in making a decision to move.
- Make sure you consider the opportunity to satisfy your needs in the new location or community.
- Don't burn your bridges. Have a back-up plan if your move doesn't work out.

PART 3

Life Goal Planning Workshop

WORKSHOP INSTRUCTIONS

In a sense, this book does not have a definite ending. It ends when you find activities in re-tirement that you consider worthwhile and enjoyable, and this will happen at different times for different people. We have however, reached a point of transition from theory to practice, so I will use this juncture to describe briefly where we are heading.

In pointing out the main drawbacks of re-tirement such as social losses, feeling of boredom, reduced motivation, and so on, keep two things in mind. First, most of the re-tirees in our sample felt that life in re-tirement was as good as or better than life before re-tirement, and most were very or reasonably satisfied with re-tirement. Second, if you are concerned about any of these drawbacks, the Life Goal Planning Workshop includes the tools to help you turn things around.

Understanding the theory behind a worthwhile and enjoyable re-tirement is only the first step. To benefit from your newfound knowledge, you have to apply it in the real world. You had a very brief look at the Life Goal Planning Workshop in Chapter 3, and now I encourage you to complete it yourself on your own or preferably with a group of friends and relatives. You can go through the exercises before or after you re-tire, and once you complete the workshop, keep working at it.

Adding items to your Life Goal List is like gathering clues to solve a mystery. Initially you gather everything that might be remotely related without judging or evaluating, and then when you sort through your clues you might see a pattern that solves the mystery. Finding worthwhile and enjoyable replacements for work may not exactly be a mystery, but I am sure you get the point. Get together with friends and family to run your own brain-storming session. On the other hand, you could brainstorm some ideas to yourself when you are alone stuck in traffic. Keep your eyes and ears open to new ideas. Watch for how you can add your personal touch to change a humdrum idea into one that is just right for you.

Creating your personal re-tirement Life Goal Plan involves written exercises and a brainstorming session, and you can complete it on your own, or preferably with a small group of friends and relatives. The process of finding worthwhile and enjoyable re-tirement pursuits applies before and after re-tirement, and although the instructional text focuses on the former, if you are re-tired you can interpret it to your situation.

The worksheets are included at the end of the book and numbered from W-1 to W-17. If you are working with a small group, you have permission to photocopy the worksheets for each participant providing you do not use it for commercial use such as in a workshop hosted by an employer, union, or financial organization. Your re-tirement strategy includes the following steps:

1. Calculate Your Re-tirement Lifestyle Readiness Score
2. List Your Re-tirement Plans
3. Identify Your Life Goal
4. Evaluate Your Re-tirement Plans
5. Brainstorm New Plans
6. After the Brainstorming
7. Guide Your Re-tirement Career

Step 1: Calculate Your Re-tirement Lifestyle Readiness Score

If you haven't already done so, start by completing the Re-tirement Lifestyle Readiness Quiz on pages W-2 to W-4. This will establish your starting point. Later when you complete the program you can re-do the quiz to see how much your lifestyle readiness has increased.

Step 2: List Your Re-tirement Plans

Next, write your re-tirement plans on page W-5. How do you plan to spend your time in re-tirement? What activities do you plan to pursue? If you are re-tired, list the activities you pursue. It doesn't matter if your plans are concrete or vague, include them anyway, and write them in your worksheets on the top of page W-5.

Step 3: Identify Your Life Goal

Your personal Life Goal is your re-tirement wish list that includes your needs, skills, and interests that you wish to satisfy when you re-tire and is the foundation upon which you will create your re-tirement. It establishes the conditions to ensure that your re-tirement will be worthwhile and enjoyable, and it will be the basis for evaluating and creating new plans. You can identify your Life Goal by answering six simple questions and writing your answers on your Life Goal Sheet starting on page W-6 in the column headed "Life Goal."

Question 1. Needs Satisfied by Work: In Chapter 2, Dave and Diane listed the things they might miss from work when they re-tire, and I asked you to do the same. If you completed this, write your replies to your Life Goal List on page W-6. If you did not complete page W-5, think about this question now. For example, you might miss friendships, routine, challenge, money, stimulation and so on. If you are re-tired, list the things you miss. The things you might miss are in fact your needs satisfied by work and given that the key to re-tirement happiness is to satisfy these needs, it is very important that you identify these needs.

Question 2. Work Skills: After listing your needs satisfied by work, on the next available lines on page W-6, list the skills you have developed through work. These can be job specific such as writing, public speaking, computer skills, etc., and you are encouraged to include general skills, such as being good with people, time management, leadership, organizational skills, and so on. These are important because part of the reason we enjoy an activity is because it gives us the opportunity to use and develop our skills, and skills are transferable. Therefore, by identifying your skills at work, you may be able to transfer these to a re-tirement activity.

Question 3. Needs Satisfied by Leisure: Having looked at work, now look at leisure. On the next available line list a current leisure activity, and below it list several reasons (one reason per line) why you enjoy it. Your reasons for enjoying leisure are in fact your needs satisfied by leisure, and together with your needs satisfied by work, they can provide important clues to your re-tirement happiness.

Question 4. Needs Satisfied by Leisure in the Past: This question is similar to question 3, but think about your leisure in the past. Include a leisure activity from the past when you were a kid or before you started working full-time, and then list your reasons for enjoying that activity. Even though you may no longer participate in some past leisure activities, listing the reasons you enjoyed them can identify additional needs.

Question 5. Leisure Skills: Think about the skills you have that you use in the context of your leisure. For example, you might include specific skills such as carpentry, painting, gardening, cooking, or more general skills such as a good listener, or a good letter writer. List any leisure skills that are not already on your list from question 2. Include what others have said you are good at even if these skills seem trivial to you. Put modesty aside and include everything you can think of.

Question 6. Re-tirement Needs: List the things you look forward to when you re-tire but are not already on your list. Your additions may include things like freedom, sleeping-in, travel, more time with your spouse/friends, no hassles, and so on. If you are re-tired, list anything else you enjoy about re-tirement.

Once you complete your Life Goal List, it should look something like the condensed example in Figure 10-1.

Figure 10-1

Life Goal	Plan A
Money	
Stimulation	
Friendships	
Efficient	
Computer Skills	
Writing	
Handyman	
Work with hands	
Holiday	
Relaxation	
Basic home repairs	
Cooking	
Bicycle	
Exploring	
No hassles	
More time with spouse	

W-6

Now answer this question. If all the items in your Life Goal List were met in re-tirement, would your re-tirement be worthwhile and enjoyable? I suspect your answer is yes because your list includes your needs, skills, and interests and if these were satisfied in re-tirement, of course it would be worthwhile and enjoyable. Your Life Goal List is very important. It is your re-tirement objective and it identifies the conditions that are necessary for your re-tirement to be worthwhile and enjoyable. It is a measuring rod should you need to make changes or improve things, and it will prove valuable should you want to come up with new ideas or plans for re-tirement.

You can also use it as a benchmark to see how your plans match up, because if they don't, later you will learn how to improve them. Now you can put your Life Goal List to work by testing your re-tirement plans.

Step 4: Evaluate Your Re-tirement Plans

Your Life Goal List outlines the conditions for a worthwhile and enjoyable re-tirement; therefore, you can use it to test your re-tirement plans. Start by thinking about the plans you wrote on page W-5, refer to your Life Goal List, and ask yourself if each item on your list will meet your re-tirement plans to your satisfaction. Write your responses in the column under Plan A. You can answer 'Y' (Yes), for those items that you expect will be met, 'N' (No), for those you do not expect will be met, or '?' (Question mark) for those you are not sure about and have to wait until you re-tire. Think about all your re-tirement plans together, not just a single activity.

For example, suppose my re-tirement plans included spending the winters in a warmer climate, my wife and I were planning to take up tennis, and I thought about finding a part-time job. I look at the first item on my list, (Figure 10-1) money, and conclude that my pension is adequate, but with the current economic situation, I am not sure if it will be enough and I may not find a part-time job, so I will mark it with a question mark. Next, I think my need for friendships will be met so I mark it with a 'Y', and so on. This is an important part of Life Goal Planning so be honest with yourself; if you do not think an item will be met, identify it appropriately as in the example in Figure 10-2.

Life Goal Shortfall

Having tested your re-tirement plans, if you identified any items that will not be met in re-tirement, you have a shortfall in meeting your Life Goal. List on page W-12, the items that are important to you and that you would like to maintain in re-tirement but that you designated with "N" or "?"

To return to my plans, one thing I have learned is my main reason for thinking about a part-time job is to satisfy my need for stimulation and challenge, more so than the money. So I don't want just any job, I want one that will satisfy these needs. What have you learned about your plans?

Figure 10-2

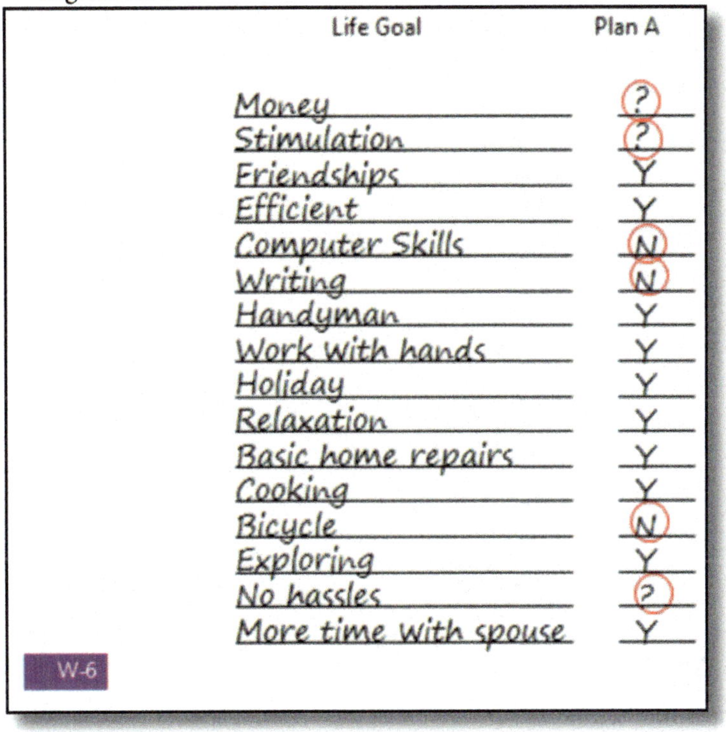

Compare Different Plans

If you are considering two different re-tirement plans, for example finding another job or sticking with your original re-tirement plan, you can evaluate and compare different scenarios. You can use the Plan B column to evaluate finding a job, and compare it with your original Plan A (see Figure 10-3). This example assumes that you have a specific job in mind and are able to determine if it will satisfy your needs and skills. If you do not have a particular job in mind, you may have to include several question marks when evaluating certain Life Goal items such as stimulation, challenge, and so on. Comparing the results may make it obvious which plan is likely to satisfy more of your needs and skills, and hence be more worthwhile and enjoyable.

If you completed the exercises, you have identified your re-tirement objective or your Life Goal, so you know the conditions that will make your re-tirement worthwhile and enjoyable. You have used this valuable information to test your re-tirement plans so you know the quality of your plans, whether they will enable you to reach your Life Goal, and if not, the areas that could be improved. You have also

Figure 10-3

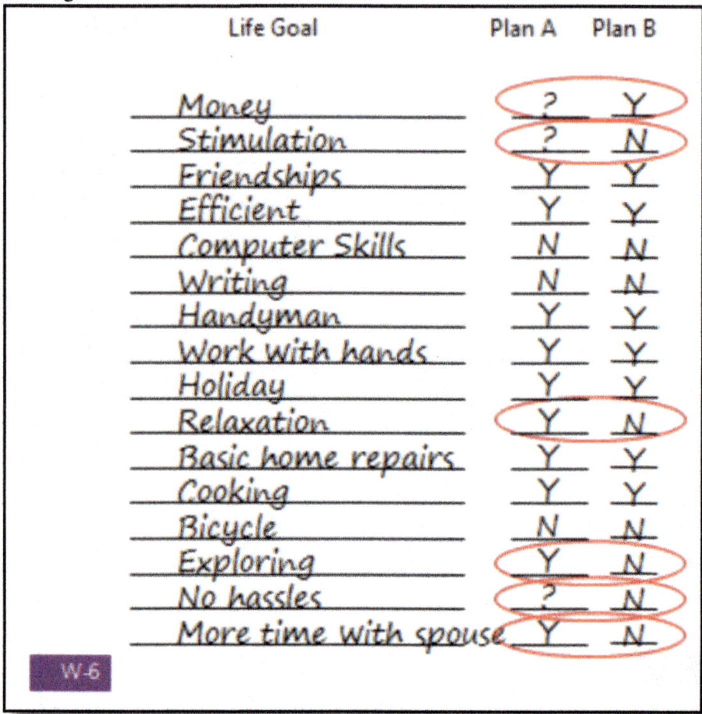

learned how to compare re-tirement plans. You are well ahead of others who do not know where they are heading.

Step 5: Brainstorm New Plans

Even if your plans look like they will enable you to reach your Life Goal, conditions could change, they may lose their appeal after the initial euphoria of the '*honeymoon stage*' wears off, or you may not have a solid re-tirement plan to begin with. If you are re-tired and feel something is missing, you may be looking for new interests. Whatever your situation now or in the future, the perfect re-tirement activities will not fall into your lap and you have to start somewhere. The best way to start this process is through a brainstorming session and the purpose is to come up with as many initial suggestions or ideas as possible as a starting point for your re-tirement career. You can complete the brainstorming on your own, but it can be much more effective if it is completed with a group as group members make re-tirement suggestions to each other. Get your spouse, friends, and relatives together for the

Figure 10-4

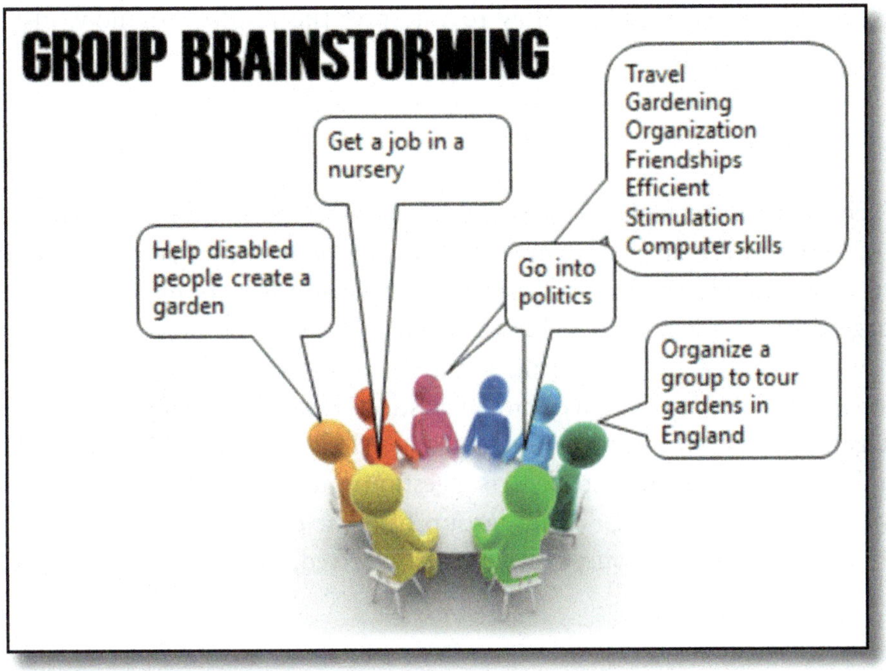

session. The others do not have to complete a Life Goal List to help you out, but if they complete their own lists, you can all take turns brainstorming with each other.

Here's how it works. If we have a group of eight people and if Peter starts, he reads his Life Goal List out loud (Figure 10-4). Meanwhile, the others are each taking notes and writing down what they consider Peter's important needs, skills, and interests. When Peter has finished reading his Life Goal List aloud, each person looks at their brainstorming notes and ties together two or three of Peter's needs, skills, and interests in order to suggest an activity for Peter in re-tirement. For example, if Peter mentioned travel, gardening, good organizer, and "I like the people I work with," Debbie might suggest that he organizes a group to tour gardens in England; Paul might suggest that he gets a job at a garden shop, Sally might suggest he help disabled people create a garden, and so on.

Suggestions Received

When suggestions are made, the reader writes the suggestions received on his or her worksheet on page W-10. Do not judge or eliminate a suggestion because it does not appeal to you or you do not think you can do it - just write it down as given. Later you will be instructed on how to interpret the results. For now, just write it down.

Suggestions Given

When each person makes a suggestion, he or she must write the suggestion he or she gave to the reader on their own worksheets on page W-11. Later you will learn the benefits of writing down your suggestion. Each person is responsible to make at least one suggestion for the person seeking re-tirement ideas. The suggestions do not have to be perfect. This is just a starting point. When making a suggestion, do not ask questions, elaborate on or justify your suggestion. Keep the discussion to a minimum but suggest what you think might satisfy the reader's needs and skills when he or she re-tires. Try to come up with realistic suggestions, and remember - anything goes, be creative, use lateral thinking. With a group of eight people, each person should end up with at least 14 suggestions; 7 suggestions received, and 7 suggestions given.

Group Facilitator

Each person is to take a turn, and work in a 10-minute time limit, to read, receive, and write his or her suggestions. Pick a timekeeper to ensure that the time limit is adhered to and that both the person who receives and makes a suggestion writes it on their *Suggestions Given* and *Suggestions Received* sheet.

Brainstorm on Your Own

To complete this stage on your own you will be wearing two hats - you will be brainstorming re-tirement career suggestions to yourself. The key here is to pretend that the Life Goal List you developed earlier belongs to someone else. Read it and removing yourself, be objective, identify or single out key or important needs and skills. Then brainstorm a few suggestions for re-tirement that you think will satisfy those needs and skills. Try to be totally objective and let the ideas flow. Put aside for the moment your likes, dislikes, abilities, and limitations. Remember, you are brainstorming for a different person. When brainstorming ideas, anything goes. Be creative, use lateral thinking, and suggest what you think might satisfy some of the needs and skills on the list. Every suggestion has the potential of providing you with a clue to enhance your enjoyment in re-tirement. When you make a suggestion, write it on page W-11.

Step 6: After the Brainstorming

The main purpose of the brainstorming is to serve as a starting point for improving or creating new plans. Nevertheless, as a valuable secondary benefit it can provide insights to add items to your Life Goal List. We will look first at expanding your Life Goal List.

Now I will let you in on a little secret. Look at page W-11, the suggestions you made to others. You may not realize this, but these suggestions can include very important clues for your benefit and this is why earlier I stressed the importance of writing down both the Suggestions Given and Received. What do you see? Likely, you see some suggestions that appeal to you. The reason for this is when you are making a suggestion to someone else, you are imposing your own interests and needs on that person, and in essence, you are saying, "If I were you, this is what I would do." In fact, you are not that other person, but you may be able to find some important clues among the suggestions you made to that other person. Do you see any suggestions or parts of suggestions that appeal to you? Do you see any patterns in the suggestions you made for others? Did you make several suggestions that involved for example, starting a business, teaching, helping others, or joining something?

If you identify any items, suggestions, or patterns that appeal to you from the suggestions you made to others, add them to your Life Goal List, if they are not already there. Then ask yourself if these additional items will help meet your re-tirement plans. If not, and if they are important to you, include them with your Life Goal Shortfall List on page W-12, and think about how you can improve your plans so that some of these newly identified needs or skills will be met.

For example, I met a welder in a workshop whose re-tirement plans included moving to a farm and opening a welding shop to keep his skills up and earn extra money. During the brainstorming, he made several suggestions to others that involved teaching in areas that focused on the individuals' interests. When he realized this hidden insight, he thought about changing his plans to see if he could somehow teach welding either through the local school or if not, maybe he could teach somebody informally in his workshop. The point is, the idea of teaching had not occurred to him until he made suggestions to others. Can you find any hidden clues in your suggestions to others?

Also, take a close look at your *Suggestions Received* on page W-10 to see if you can identify any items, suggestions, or patterns that appeal to you. If so, add them to your Life Goal List, and think about how you can improve your plans to meet some of these newly identified needs or skills.

Visualization Exercise

Another exercise that might help to expand your Life Goal List is to select an activity from all the suggestions that appeal to you from the suggestions received and given, and even if it is unrealistic, imagine you are involved in that activity. Ask yourself what you would enjoy about that activity or what needs and skills that activity would satisfy. If you identify any that are not already on you list, add them to your list. Although the activity you are visualizing may be unrealistic, it may reveal additional needs or skills that may be satisfied through a more realistic activity. For example, I recall one workshop participant who visualized being a conductor in a symphony orchestra. When she thought about why she would enjoy this activity, she listed things like being the boss, travel, loving music, and so on. She was then able to add a few of these items to her Life Goal List, which actually gave her a different perspective on her re-tirement. If you added any items to your Life Goal List, ask yourself if these additional items will meet your re-tirement plans. If not, and if they are important to you, add them to your Life Goal Shortfall List (W-12), and ask yourself how you can improve your plans so that some of these new needs or skills will be met.

Step 7: Guide Your Re-tirement Career

The main purpose of the brainstorming is to come up with as many initial suggestions or ideas as a starting point to improve or create new re-tirement plans. During the brainstorming exercise, you were asked to put personal judgments and evaluations aside to allow ideas to flow. Now you can look more closely at the results. If you identified a Life Goal shortfall with your re-tirement plans (page W-12), or if after you re-tire you feel that something is missing, you are probably looking for some new ideas to broaden your plans to satisfy those needs. You have to start somewhere so take a close look at all the suggestions you received and gave, and start with the one that has the most appeal. It may not be prefect, but it is a start.

When you re-tire if you are able to pursue activities that satisfy all your needs, you will go directly to your destination. However, things don't always work out that way. As explained earlier, re-tirement is a career that develops and evolves and to understand this process, consider the case of sailing a boat. When you go sailing, you know your destination. What you don't know is the route you will take - that depends on the wind direction. More than likely you have to tack or zigzag to reach your destination. In this way, you will discover your route, en route. Your re-tirement career will probably be similar. Your objective or destination is to satisfy the items on your

Life Goal List but you may have to discover your actual route, en route as you progress through the various activities that ultimately make up your re-tirement career. Here's how it works.

As illustrated in Figure 10-5, start with your re-tirement plan; it could be your original plans or a suggestion from the brainstorming session. We can call this Plan A, and suppose after you re-tire you find that something is missing. To discover what is missing, consult your Life Goal List, select another column, and evaluate each item on your list against your current experience. This will give you an idea of what is missing or how far you are from your Life Goal. Once you identify the items that are missing, brainstorm a new plan - Plan B. You are now basing your brainstorming on your experience with Plan A, and therefore you may come up with something quite new that you might not have thought of before you experienced Plan A. If your next plan is still not perfect, continue the process until eventually you will reach your destination and by finding re-tirement activities that meet your needs and skills. This way you will be guiding your re-tirement career.

To return to my hypothetical example, my Plan A was to spend the winters in a warmer climate, my wife and I were planning to take up tennis, and I thought about finding a part-time job, not necessarily for the money, but for the challenge and stimulation. Suppose after I re-tire my plan did not quite work out. I couldn't find a suitable part-time job and although we enjoy being away in the winter, I sprained my ankle playing tennis, and I am a bit bored. There is something missing from my life. To improve my situation I look back at my Life Goal List and identified friendships as one thing that was missing so we decided to join a tennis club to take lessons and to meet new people. There we met a couple who invited us to go hiking. We have never hiked before but decided to join them. It turns out we had a great time with their group on the hike and we spent most weekends hiking. At one point, I volunteered to organize a hiking trip for the group to Europe, and it was a great success. This became my Plan B (a revised Plan A) in Figure 10-5. Based on the success of our Europe trip I developed a Web site that included an active chat room and I started to organize hiking trips to exotic locations. Now I am earning extra money through an activity I find challenging and stimulating, we are traveling to scout out potential hiking trips and, lo and behold, I have reached my destination and am satisfying all my needs. In fact, I am satisfying more needs now than before I re-tired. In this sense, I discovered my route to re-tirement happiness, en route.

This process can take place before or after you re-tire. Depending on your plans, do your homework, talk to people who are involved in it, read about it, do whatever it takes to find out more about that activity. In the process, and here is the key, you

Figure 10-5

might come up with another and perhaps more realistic or appealing idea that would have never occurred to you had you not started your investigation.

With my hypothetical example, if before I re-tired someone had suggested that I sell exotic hiking trips online when I re-tire, I would have rejected it outright as a ridiculous suggestion. But because I couldn't find a part-time job that was stimulating, was missing friendships, sprained my ankle, and was bored, that led to joining the tennis club, which led to meeting a couple of hikers, and so on. This may take some work on your part and it may take time, but remember, your needs, skills, and interests are unique and you have to get out there to find or create your ideal re-tirement that meets all the conditions on your Life Goal List.

Continue the Process

I encourage you to continue the process. Keep adding items to your Life Goal List by thinking about the six questions listed at the beginning of this chapter, and continue to brainstorm new ideas with your friends, family, and on your own. Finding worthwhile and enjoyable replacements for work is your key to re-tirement happiness, and the workshop is the vehicle that will enable this process. For some it may take time, while for others, it may not be necessary. You have everything to gain and nothing to lose by completing and thinking about the exercises.

Additional Exercises

The Decision to Re-tire

If you are grappling with the decision to re-tire, here are two additional exercises. Begin by clarifying your reasons for re-tiring. On page W-13, under the Push column, answer the following question, "When I re-tire I am happy to give up......" Your list should include things you don't like about your work. These can include anything from some of the people you work with, the nature of the task, the hours, location, dress code, politics, and so on. There should be no reference to re-tirement on this list. Just think about the problems or negative aspects of your work. Spend a little time with this and add, as many things as you can to your '*Push*' list, no matter how mundane they may seem.

Next, turn to the '*Pull*' column. For this exercise you can forget about work and list the things you look forward to when you no longer have to work by answering the following question, "When I re-tire I am looking forward to...." Even if you do not have solid plans for re-tirement, list the things you expect to enjoy in re-tirement. Your list may include things like freedom, sleeping in, travel, more time with my wife/husband/friends, working in my garden, and so on.

Take a hard look at your '*Push*' and '*Pull*' lists, and compare them. It doesn't matter which list includes more items, the important consideration is to weigh one list against the other. By listing your reasons for leaving or staying at work, it may become clear if you based your decision mainly on push or pull factors. Ideally, you should base the decision to re-tire mainly on pull considerations.

Compare Work and Re-tirement

You learned how to evaluate your future plans by determining if you could meet each of your needs and skills in re-tirement. You can apply this same process to assist you with the decision to re-tire. Here's how this works. The column on the left side of your Life Goal List is headed Current Life. Ask yourself whether your current work and leisure is meeting each item on your list to your satisfaction. You are not thinking about your future re-tirement, but are concentrating on your current life. Respond to each item with "Y" (yes this item is being met) or "N" (no, it is not being met). You are evaluating a current experience, so there are no question marks in this evaluation.

When this is completed, compare all the data you gathered so far; your needs and skills met through your current work and leisure, your needs and skills you expect to meet when you re-tire, and your '*Push*' and '*Pull*' lists. With this information in front of you, if you find work is meeting more of your important needs and skills compared to your pending re-tirement, and that your '*Pull*' list is limited, clearly, you are not ready to re-tire. Re-tirement may be a case of going from the frying pan to the fire. It might end up being worse than staying at work (if you have the choice). Having said that, as everyone re-tires eventually, you must change the balance, in favor of your '*pull*' considerations. You must get on with the job of finding activities in re-tirement that will be worthwhile and enjoyable.

Alternatively, if the opposite should take place, if your '*pull*' considerations are substantive and if it appears that more of your needs and skills will be met in re-tirement than in your current work, there is a strong indication that re-tirement is the preferable route to go. Ideally, you should make this decision independently from financial considerations.

Creating Activities Together

Say we have two people, Jef and Monica, who want to get involved in a new activity together but have no idea where to start. First Jef brings out his Needs and Skill List. Monica peruses Jef's list and identifies items on his list that she could apply to herself. They write these items on a separate Needs and Skills List. Next, Jef peruses Monica's list and transfers items that could apply to him to the new list. In so doing, they create a combined Needs and Skills List that includes items that apply to both of them. It will probably be shorter than their own lists as all the items on the combined list have to apply to both Jef and Monica. With their combined Needs and Skills List, Jef and Monica can begin to brainstorm suggestions to develop or create an activity that will appeal to them both. The process will be identical to that described earlier, only in this case it involves two people.

Single in Re-tirement

This issue was addressed in Chapter 8. If you are single before or after you re-tire, and if you feel this can affect your re-tirement happiness, start by adding 'being single' to your Life Goal List. And then, evaluate your plans or try to create new plans based on this additional condition.

If you become single after you re-tire, and if you feel this is affecting your ret-irement, go back to your Life Goal List, add this element, and reinterpret your current plans based on this new addition. One obvious issue in this context could be friendships. You may want to put extra emphasis on this need when evaluating or creating new re-tirement plans.

Figure 10-4

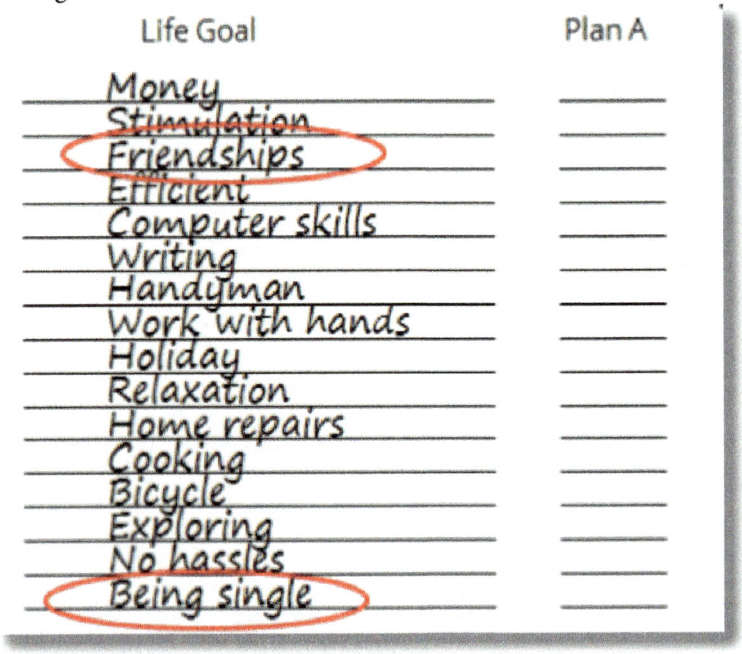

LIFE GOAL PLANNING WORKSHEETS

Retirement Lifestyle Readiness Quiz

Please circle the number between 1 and 7 which best describes how that statement (if

A) Attitude Toward Retirement

1. How do you feel about the prospect of retiring?	I dread the thought	1 2 3 4 5 6 7	Looking forward to it/can't wait
2. In general, would you say retirement has a positive or a	Very negative	1 2 3 4 5 6 7	Totally positive
3. Would you say that most people associate retirement	Most definitely	1 2 3 4 5 6 7	Absolutely not

B) Spending Time

4. Do you have solid plans for retirement?	None/haven't thought about it	1 2 3 4 5 6 7	I know exactly what I want to do
5. Do you have a contingency plan if your first plan doesn't work	None/haven't thought about it	1 2 3 4 5 6 7	Yes, no problem
6. If you are thinking about working in retirement, would your main reasons be financial	Strictly financial	1 2 3 4 5 6 7	Strictly non-financial

C) Decision to Retire

7. When you retire, what will your decision be based on?	No longer enjoying my job/work	1 2 3 4 5 6 7	Have things I prefer to do in retirement

D) Spousal Relations (if applicable)

8. Have you discussed your retirement plans with your spouse?	No we haven't discussed it	1 2 3 4 5 6 7	Totally aware
9. Is your spouse looking forward to your retirement?	No	1 2 3 4 5 6 7	Yes

E) Housing (If applicable)

10. Do you plan to move after	Have plans	1 2 3 4 5 6 7	No plans at this time
11. Do you have a contingency	No/haven't thought about it	1 2 3 4 5 6 7	Yes

F) Friendships

12. Do most of your friends come	Strictly from work	1 2 3 4 5 6 7	Strictly outside work
13. When you retire, will most of	Yes most will be working	1 2 3 4 5 6 7	No most will be retired

G) Miss From Work

14. What (if anything) do you expect to miss from no longer being involved in your current

Social interaction	Keeping busy	Other ____________________
Sense of achievement	Routine	____________________
Challenges	Keeping current	____________________
Contribution	Status in the community	____________________
Involvement	Responsibility	____________________
		____________________

Calculate Your Re-tirement Lifestyle Readiness Score

Total the scores for each section and divide by the number of questions answered in that section. For example, in Section A, if you answered three questions with 6, 4, & 2, your total score is 12 and your average is 12/3 = 4. In Section B, if you answered 2 out of 3 questions (6, 5), your total score is 11 and your average is 11/2=5.5.

If you scored less than 5 on any section, you have identified an area that requires

	Total Score	Average Score
A) Attitude Toward Re-tirement	____________	____________
B) Spending Time	____________	____________
C) Decision to Re-tire	____________	____________
D) Spousal Relationships	____________	____________
E) Housing	____________	____________
F) Friendships	____________	____________
G) Miss from Work	____________	____________

My Re-tirement Plans

Life Goal	Plan A	Plan B

Plan C	Plan D	Plan E	Plan F	Plan G
________	________	________	________	________
________	________	________	________	________
________	________	________	________	________
________	________	________	________	________
________	________	________	________	________
________	________	________	________	________
________	________	________	________	________
________	________	________	________	________
________	________	________	________	________
________	________	________	________	________
________	________	________	________	________
________	________	________	________	________
________	________	________	________	________
________	________	________	________	________

Life Goal	Plan A	Plan B

Plan C	Plan D	Plan E	Plan F	Plan G
________	________	________	________	________
________	________	________	________	________
________	________	________	________	________
________	________	________	________	________
________	________	________	________	________
________	________	________	________	________
________	________	________	________	________
________	________	________	________	________
________	________	________	________	________
________	________	________	________	________
________	________	________	________	________
________	________	________	________	________
________	________	________	________	________
________	________	________	________	________

Suggestions Received

1____

2____

3____

4____

5____

6____

7____

8____

Suggestions Given
(Brainstorming on your own)

1 ______________________________

____

2 ______________________________

____

3 ______________________________

____

4 ______________________________

____

5 ______________________________

____

6 ______________________________

____

7 ______________________________

____

8 ______________________________

____

Life Goal Shortfall

The Decision to Re-tire

Push Factors	Pull Factors
______	______
______	______
______	______
______	______
______	______
______	______
______	______
______	______
______	______
______	______
______	______
______	______
______	______
______	______
______	______
______	______

Incorporate Life Goal with Financial Planning

The more information you have about how you plan to spend time in retirement (Life Goal Planning), the more likely will you or your adviser be able to identify your financial goal and develop a personalized plan based on your future financial needs. To share this information with your wealth adviser, complete pages W-14 to W-17.

My Life Goal Plan

Plan A

____

____

____

Financial Implications ____________________________

____

____

Plan B

____

____

____

Financial Implications ____________________________

____

____

Plan C

Financial Implications

Plan D

Financial Implications

Plan E

Financial Implications

2) Unfulfilled Needs: Important needs or skills that will not be met given my future plans (W-12)

3) Plans that have the most appeal from my brainstorming exercise (pages W-10 and W-11).

1____

2____

3____

4____

5____

6____

7____

8____

Life After Dentistry Survey Questions

This survey is for dentists who are retired, or have elected to continue to practice dentistry on a part-time basis. It can be completed in less then 15 minutes. Thank you for taking part. Your anonymous responses will be a valuable resource for other dentists in their transition to retirement. Note, the use of the word 'retired' in the survey questions refers also to semi-retired.

PART 1: Retirement Plans and Preparation

1. How would you describe your participation in dentistry?
2. At what age did you retire (semi-retire) from practicing dentistry?
3. How long have you been retired (semi-retired) from practicing dentistry?
4. Did you retire by choice or were there factors beyond your control that forced you to retire?
5. Why did you retire when you did?
6. If you could do it over, would you still retire at the same age?
7. As best you can recall, how did you feel about the prospect of retiring just before you actually retired?
8. Did you receive any formal pre-retirement planning assistance before you retired?

   7a. Who provided the pre-retirement planning?

   7b. What did the pre-retirement planning include?
9. Is there any area of retirement planning that you now wish you had given more attention?
10. Looking back, how thorough were you at preparing for retirement?

PART 2: Spending Time In Retirement

11. List the main Leisure (non-work) activities you pursue in retirement.
12. Since retiring, have you ever worked for salary or other compensation?

    11a. Before retiring, did you expect to work for salary or other compensation?

    11b. Is/was your work in after retirement part-time or full-time?

    11c. Is/was your work in retirement related to dentistry?

11d. Was your main reason for working after you retired mostly financial or non-financial?

11e. What were the main non-financial reasons for working in retirement?

13. Since retiring have you been involved with any unpaid voluntary or charitable activity?

12a. Describe the voluntary or charitable activity.

12b. Were you involved in charitable activities before you retired?

12c. Were the charitable activities you pursued before you retired the same or different from those you pursued in retirement?

PART 3: Housing and Location

14. Did retirement prompt you to move?

13a. Why did you move at or following retirement?

13b. Did you move far enough away that you had to establish new friends?

13c. Any advice for people who are thinking about moving after retirement?

PART 4: Impressions and Advice

15. Everything considered, how would you compare life after retirement to life before retirement?
16. What (if anything) do you miss from no longer working full-time?
17. In general, how satisfied are you with your retirement?
18. What are the main attractions or benefits of retirement?
19. What (if any) are the main drawbacks or disadvantages of retirement?
20. In general, what advice would you give to other dentists who are approaching retirement?

PART 5: General information

21. Your gender?
22. Your present age?
23. In general, how would you describe your health?
24. Your present marital status.
25. Type of practice.
26. Where did you practice dentistry?

References

Introduction

1. Roadburg, Alan, Ph.D., Aging: Retirement, Work and Leisure, Methuen Publications, Toronto, 1985.
2. AARP Research, Retirement Security or Insecurity? The Experience of Workers Aged 45 and Older, Colette Thayer, Ph.D., AARP Knowledge Management, October 2008.
3. Desjardines Financial, Rethinking Retirement Survey, 2008.
4. Financial Planning Association Web site (www.fpanet.org)

Chapter 1

1. W.I. Thomas and D.S. Thomas. The Child in America: Behavior Problems and Programs. New York: Knopf, 1928, 571-572.
2. Virshup B, Coombs RH, Physicians' Adjustment to Retirement, Western Journal of Medicine 1993 Feb; 158:142-144
3. Scott Highhouse, quoted in The Globe and Mail, June 3, 2011.

Chapter 4

1. Transamerica Center for Retirement Studies, Redefining Retirement: The 'New Retirement Readiness' May 2012
2. Employee Benefit Research Institute and Mathew Greenwald & Associates, Changing Expectations About Retirement, Retirement Confidence Survey, 2012
3. The SunAmerica Retirement Re-Set Study: Redefining Retirement Post Recession, 2011, www.retirementreset.com
4. www.cbc.ca/news/business/story/2012/08/20/cibc-retirement-survey.html
5. Allstate and Matthew Greenwald & Associates, Retirement Reality Check, 2004.
6. Pew Research Center, Working After Retirement: The Gap Between Expectations and Reality, 2006.

Chapter 7

1. Bolles, Richard N., The Three Boxes of Life, Ten Speed Press, Berkeley CA, 1981, 354
2. Doidge, Norman, M.D., The Brain that Changes Itself, Penguin Books, 2007. See also Elkhonon Goldberg, Ph.D., The Wisdom Paradox, Gotham Books, 2005.
3. American Academy of Anti-Aging Medicine, The World Health Network, Keeping Ageing Brains On Top Form, 2005.
4. Walton, Mark, Boundless Potential: Transform Your Brain, Unleash Your Talents, Reinvent Your Work in Midlife and Beyond, McGraw-Hill, 2012.

Photo Credits

Introduction

depositphotos.com
6540395

Chapter 1

depositphotos.com
4878091

Chapter 2

depositphotos.com
4878361

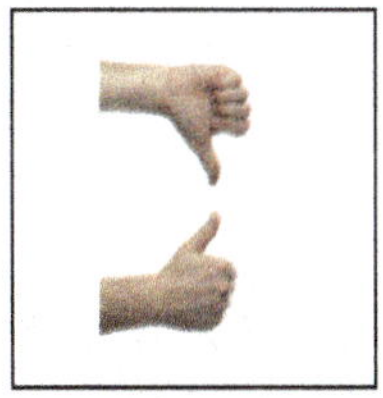

depositphotos.com
11949444

Chapter 3

depositphotos.com
10717064

depositphotos.com
1370068

Chapter 4

yaymicro.com
1718759

depositphotos.com
8381384

Chapter 5

depositphotos.com
10584663

Chapter 6

depositphotos.com
5999323

Chapter 7

yaymicro.com
4136752

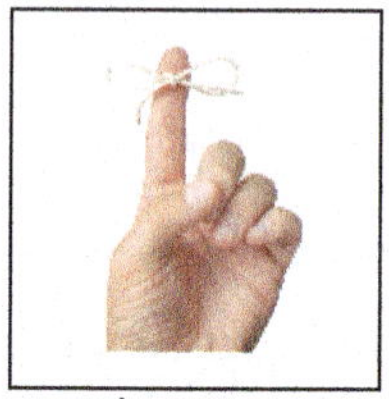

yaymicro.com
2611541

depositphotos.com
5722133

Chapter 8

istockphoto.com
3471179

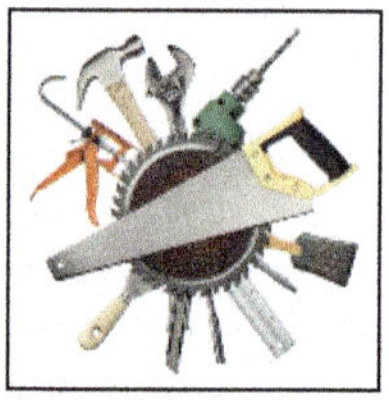

depositphotos.com
9849358

Chapter 9

depositphotos.com
1039573

istockphoto.com
9066188

Workshop

yaymicro.com
481132

depositphotos.com
9458664

CPSIA information can be obtained
at www.ICGtesting.com
Printed in the USA
BVOW07s0743200117
474030BV00025B/114/P